Surface Bait Subtleties

Topwater Tactics For Muskies

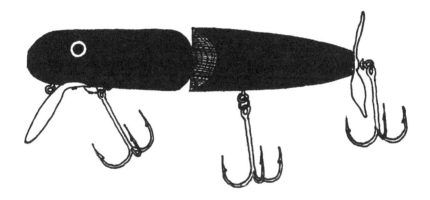

By John Dettloff

Published by:

Musky Hunter Publications

Minocqua, Wisconsin
(715) 356-6301,
an imprint of:

WILLOW CREEK PRESS

Minocqua, Wisconsin

Cover art by:
Garett Shipman
452B Billings Ave.
Medford, WI 54451
(715) 748-2516
Prints are available from the artist

Library of Congress Number Cataloging-in-Publication Data
Dettloff, John.
    Surface bait subtleties : topwater tactics for muskies / by John Dettloff.
      p. cm.
    ISBN 1-57223-028-2
    1. Muskellunge fishing. 2. Lure fishing. I. Title.
    SH691.M8D47   1995
    799.1'753—dc20   95-18265
                                       CIP

Printed in the United States of America

Contents

Acknowledgements

James Heddon — inventor, publisher, and former mayor of Dowagiac, Michigan, probably deserves as much credit for the development of the surface bait as anyone. The story of how Heddon came up with the idea to create wooden surface baits has been told many times over and has long been rooted in angling folklore. The story, considered to be very credible, occurred over a century ago.

As accounted in the book, *The Collector's Guide to Antique Fishing Tackle*, the story goes: "Heddon, waiting for a fishing friend, was passing the time in idle whittling. Done, or maybe when the friend arrived, he tossed the wooden "plug" into the lake — where upon a bass attacked it with enough verve to make Heddon sit up and take notice. By about 1890, he was carving purpose-made wooden fishing plugs, with hooks attached. By 1901 James Heddon & Sons was in commercial production, offering fishermen the original "wooden bait," which became known as the "Dowagiac Perfect Surface Casting Bait."

And the rest, as they say, is history ...

Since then, surface baits have made up a significant part of the sport of angling and, during the past 21 seasons, have been consistently my most productive method for taking muskies. Now make no mistake, I'll use whatever lure it takes to catch a musky; but my preference will always be to use a surface bait — when the conditions allow it.

Growing up at my family's fishing resort and being surrounded by so many accomplished musky men has helped plunge me deeply into the sport of musky fishing. Men like Frenchy LaMay, Walter J. Roman, Jim Burns, Fred Hirsch, Ron Dettloff, Joe Jasek, and Bruce Tasker are responsible for both sparking my interest and contributing to my knowledge of surface bait fishing for muskies.

And lastly, I must thank my wife, Paulette, for having patiently endured an endless barrage of fish stories over the years — one of the hazards of being married to a musky guide. But then again, she's a musky fisherperson too. So maybe these stories fire her up just as much as they do me.

— JOHN DETTLOFF

The Making Of A Surface Bait Fisherman

O ur earliest musky memories are often the most fondly remembered ones, experiences that usually have the biggest impact on luring one into a lifelong love affair with the sport of musky fishing. One of my first serious musky outings was one such experience — one which solidified me into becoming, first and foremost, a surface bait fisherman.

It all started 21 years ago, back in July of 1974, when I became a surface bait devotee. And what better place to start out than on the Chippewa Flowage, one of musky country's best-known surface bait lakes, and with Frenchy LaMay, one of the flowage's most legendary topwater anglers, "showing me the ropes." This was truly a winning combination.

Surface Bait Subtleties

Our resort was putting on a little musky tournament and when Frenchy said, "I'll take Johnny as my partner," my fate became set. What a thrill for a 12-year-old, under the guidance of Frenchy, to actually go fish the very spots that — up until that point — I had only heard talked about in reverent whispers in our bar.

Armed with a five-foot solid glass rod and a red Garcia 6000 reel, I was ready. Frenchy handed me one of his (now famous) homemade lures, a black Topper, slightly oversized and with heavy gauge spinners. "Here, try this," he said. "Wow!" I thought.

I knew his lures were regarded as jewels by the other musky men — especially back then, when Frenchy was only sparingly giving them out to friends. And the muskies liked his lures, too! I remembered the BIG ONE that I weighed in for Frenchy just the season before — a near 40-pounder that fell victim to one of Frenchy's orange Toppers. (See the February/March 1991 issue of *Musky Hunter* magazine for a detailed article about Frenchy LaMay.)

Frenchy made sure that my reel was filled with braided line. "No monofilament line with surface baits," he cautioned. The reduced stretch of the braided line allows for a much better hookset, especially when a musky sinks his teeth deep into a surface lure (which predomi-

Frenchy LaMay's 39-pound 11-ounce musky caught on August 5, 1973. Note how it "engulfs" a 10-pounder caught by Jim Burns (pictured).

nately are made out of wood) greatly handicapping one's hooksetting ability. This was lesson No. 1 — a simple lesson that dramatically increases your odds of hooking a musky.

Surface Bait Subtleties

In our first spot, a stump infested bar called Knucklebuster, I anxiously hurled out and retrieved my lure. "Don't reel in too fast now," Frenchy instructed. He wanted the Topper to come in slowly, so the front prop would push a nice, easy wake and the back prop would "churgle" the water. "Big fish want a slow, easy bait," he said. This was lesson No. 2 — another very basic, but crucial, surface bait subtlety. This is a key to maximizing big fish production!

It was no time at all, it seemed, before I had a musky follow and push a nice wake behind my Topper. Frenchy then interjected, "You know if you catch one on that, you can keep the lure." With the prospect of being able to keep this prized lure fueling my enthusiasm, I didn't want to miss any chances. And when it came time to take a dinner break an hour or so later, along a protected shoreline of Eagle's Nest Island, I just scarfed down my sandwich and resumed my casting. After firing a cast next to a stump and only moving my lure a few inches, POW!

A musky hit my Topper and whitewater was soon flying all over! I later discovered that this was lesson No. 3 — the splash of your lure hitting the water is the big attractor for a musky. Most hits will come early in the retrieve and you must be ready to set the hooks when it happens!

The Making Of A Surface Bait Fisherman

Musky legend Frenchy LaMay (left) guided the author to this fish in July 1974, a catch that forever turned Dettloff into a surface bait fisherman.

As the musky went flying into the air and cart-wheeled right next to the boat, I can remember being both excited and petrified. "Maybe this could be a 20-pounder," I thought. After Frenchy subdued the fish and brought it aboard, I found out my buck fever had magnified the

Surface Bait Subtleties

musky's size a bit. But even at 31 1/2 inches, this musky was no less memorable and enough to win our little evening's contest.

It wasn't long before I began to greatly add to both my topwater arsenal and my knowledge of surface bait fishing. And being exposed to so many topwater technicians early on, put me on an immediate path to success. By taking the unique little topwater secrets that I picked up from each of the musky men I knew and combining them with all of the additional tips that I have discovered over the past 21 years, this article will pass on to you a wealth of "surface bait subtleties" that will help you maximize your topwater results.

Just How Effective Are Surface Baits, Anyway?

Too many musky hunters underestimate the effectiveness of surface lures and, all too often, can be found possessing only a spattering of token surface baits in their tackle boxes — lures which commonly collect more dust than tooth marks. Contrary to what some anglers may think, surface bait fishing for muskies is not solely restricted to just the shallow, darker water lakes and flowages, nor is it a thing of the past.

The fact is: while darker waters such as the Chippewa Flowage are likely to yield optimum topwater results, surface baits also produce very well on a wide variety of waters — including rivers, clear water natural lakes, Canadian shield lakes (Lake of the Woods, Rowan Lake, and Lac Seul to name a few), and even Georgian Bay. And on many of these waters, where subsurface has long been the rule, surface baits frequently offer the muskies something completely different. Now, while I don't consider a musky to be a creature capable of logic and reason, primordial instinct may at times make old esox a little leery of the commonly thrown lures. So it can't hurt to throw lures that these finny beasts haven't seen before.

Who would throw a subsurface bait here, anyway? This rare photo depicts the famed Chippewa Flowage in the 1940s, when standing timber was still a factor.

Surface Bait Subtleties

The perception that surface baits are a thing of the past is best explained by examining the availability factor of today's musky lures. Today, there are substantially fewer quality surface lures available on the market than there were years ago; whereas, the availability of quality jerk-baits, divers, and bucktails has dramatically increased during recent years. So while the availability factor is making surface lures less dominant in the marketplace, make no

The late "Smokey" Jandrt, a Chippewa River guide for over 50 years seen during a 1986 float trip, preferred small Toppers, Flaptails and Hawg Wobblers when it came to topwater fishing on the river.

Just How Effective Are Surface Baits, Anyway?

A black Globe attracted this nice, 46-inch musky for Bob Benson in Canada's Rowan Lake in 1991.

mistake — they are still irresistible to Mr. Musky!

Just how irresistible? Well, being a self admitted "data cruncher," let's examine just how productive surface lures have been for my guide clients and myself. Of the 499 muskies over 30 inches that I've boated during the past 21 years up to the 15th of October (what I consider the end of the prime artificial bait season), 302 or 60.5 percent were caught on surface baits and the remainder of those fish were caught primarily on bucktails and jerkbaits.

Surface Bait Subtleties

And what about big fish? The success percentage climbs even higher. Out of 23 muskies in the 25-pound class or better that I've boated within the same time frame, 17, or 74 percent, of the big fish came on surface lures. The stats help bear out what topwater musky hunters have been saying for years — surface lures are big fish baits!

Surface lures are great for the giant muskies in Canada's giant lakes. Just ask Ray Kerby, whose 40-pounder from Georgian Bay fell to a Twin Teasertail.

Equipment Tips

For me, an ideal surface bait rod ranges between 6 feet and 6 1/2 feet in length and has noticeably more stiffness than a bucktail rod. This additional stiffness is required to ensure both optimum casting results and the best possible hookset when using these heavier, usually wooden, lures. There are many fine examples of quality surface bait rods available today. Two that satisfy my needs are the Cabela's Fish Eagle graphite 6-foot-2 rod and the St. Croix Premier graphite 6-foot rod.

Baitcasting reels are essential for best surface bait casting efficiency. Anglers who try it with spinning reels run into the problem of not being able to smoothly stop the lure just before it hits the water. This inhibits both pinpoint casting accuracy and makes it difficult to eliminate the bow in your line just before your lure hits the water. (A high percentage of strikes come right after the lure hits the water, so it's crucial the bow be out of your line if you want to get a good hookset — an important tip!)

Baitcasting reels with a levelwinding mechanism

that doesn't move with the line as it's paying out are not recommended when using the heavier braided lines. It results in uneven line pile-ups on your reel, handicapping one's casting ability. The reels with a "moving levelwind" help maximize both casting ease and distance.

I have always found Garcia Ambassadeur reels (5500 C and 6500 C) to be tailor-made for this purpose. Take note that the more recent Garcia reels have a faster gear ratio and it is easy to find oneself retrieving a surface

It takes a stout rod, well-made baitcasting reel, and heavy, braided line to heft a big lure like a Globe all day.

Surface Bait Subtleties

lure too fast.

As mentioned earlier, when using surface baits, a strong, low-stretch braided line is preferred to ensure an adequate hookset. Braided lines do vary greatly in both durability and stretch, so don't let an inferior line turn what should have been the biggest musky catch of your lifetime into, well, "just another fish story."

Line color is another consideration. What's better, black or white line? Most musky hunters are quick to choose black line because, as they are looking down into the water at it, they can't see it. Actually, how it looks to them is irrelevant. What matters is how it looks to the muskies!

Well, not being able to speak fluent esox, I wasn't able to ask a musky. I had to find out for myself by donning a diving mask and observing the situation from underwater as someone cast black and white lines over my head. The less visible choice was obvious. While the black line was much more visible when looking up at it with the lighter colored sky in the background, the white line was more difficult to see — in all sky conditions. In fact, when the sky was mostly cloudy to overcast, the white line was almost invisible. Now how much line visibility matters — especially in darker water — is debatable. But one thing's for sure: if it does matter, white line is the better choice when working lures near the surface.

I have found only one line to best fulfill the three critical line requirements of durability, very low stretch and low visibility — white Cortland Micron 40-pound test. This is not mentioned for promotional purposes; this is merely a tip that will help you increase your surface bait production.

A brief comment should be made about the new

Chippewa Flowage guide Bruce Tasker (pictured in his younger days) can tell you from experience that the Globe and Topper have been two "tried and true" surface lures. One quick glance at this photo should take many people back to the "Eisenhower era." The photo also gives a look at the equipment of another time.

The man credited as the person to catch the first musky from the Chippewa Flowage, in 1923, was the late guide Harry Lessard. He took this 30-pounder on a perch Surf-Oreno in 1939.

braided microfilament lines that have recently been introduced. These lines — whether they be made with Spectra fibers, Kevlar, or copolymers — are super strong, have very low stretch, and are offered in remarkably fine diameters. Now being more from the old school, I must admit that I don't plan on giving up my Cortland Micron braided line. This line has proven itself to be top quality. But then again, these new lines certainly can't be ignored.

After testing out these new lines for myself, I have discovered three possible areas of concern. First: if you don't have these new lines tightly packed onto your reel spool, you run an increased risk of having these fine diameter lines cut and bury into your spool when the line is under heavy pressure. Second: because many of these new lines are both so fine and have a coarser weave, they are more difficult to visually inspect for nicks and frays. And third: for some reason, some of these new lines quickly fray from the repetitive abuse of casting the heavier lures.

But other than these areas of concern, these new lines undoubtedly offer some noteworthy benefits. The biggest one is that these finer diameter lines are easier to cast for the novice or intermediate musky angler. This makes these lines a great choice for the less experienced casters to use. And in clearer water conditions, where line visibility is more of a factor, these smaller diameter lines are potentially less visible to the fish as well.

As far as leaders go, I never go without one. I prefer 7- to 11-inch long, single-strand, 240-pound test stainless steel wire leaders with a good strong snap and no swivel. Why no swivel? Well, a swivel just represents another potentially weak link in your leader that may someday break and cost you a big fish. It also adds a little extra weight to your leader, weight that can help nosedive your surface bait and possibly take away some of its action. A properly working surface bait should never roll over and twist your line — therefore, a swivel serves no practical purpose when it comes to these lures and could actually serve as a handicap.

A considerable number of muskies do take surface baits down deep into their mouths — especially the larger ones that have heads as big as a small bucket! It is for these fish, and the ones that roll on your line, that you want to have a good, strong leader. I can remember back in early September of 1978 when having no leader cost a friend of mine one very huge fish. Al Becker was fishing with guide Bill Shirriff on an overcast, fishy-looking day. Al, who was throwing a Cisco Kid Topper on one of the Chippewa Flowage's many prime big fish spots, wasn't using a leader at the time. He knew he should have taken the time out to put on a leader, but for some reason just neglected to do it.

And then it happened. Al tied into the biggest musky that he and Bill had ever seen! It was a true monster, well over 40 pounds for sure — and it had inhaled the Topper. The musky was hooked solidly and Al had the fish on for quite some time. Both men got a real good look at this magnificent fish, but it was just a matter of time before the line got cut on the musky's mouth and the fish was gone.

Our resort tavern wasn't too far away from where these two men did battle with this beast of a fish so, in short order, they opted to take a break to have a cold drink at our bar. Al Becker, a mountain of a man, was livid, stamping his feet on our concrete floor and mad at himself for not taking the time out to put a leader on. There happens to be a big crack in our floor on that very spot and I wouldn't be surprised if Becker was responsible for it. Oh, maybe not. But I do know one thing for sure — Becker's ordeal taught me to never go without a leader.

Note how deeply this 36-pounder caught by John Kondrasuk in the Chippewa Flowage in 1960 inhaled the Black Globe. A long leader is an absolute must!

27

Lures

Many anglers may not realize it, but surface lures bought "off the shelf" very often are not "fine tuned" and ready to use. Not to worry though, because most of these lures can be tuned into being productive fish getters. Because quality can vary, an occasional surface lure just can't be made to work without doing a major rebuild on it. In such a case, you may think that you're stuck with just an "expensive piece of kindling," but many reputable bait shops will take such lures back. After all, they want to keep your business.

Fine tuning surface lures, so they will produce just the right sound, is one of the most important skills a top-water technician must possess. And the key to mastering this skill is to repeatedly practice tuning your lures, while making careful observations as to how your tuning alters the sound.

Some of the finest surface baits ever made are no longer in production. But, if you know where to look and are willing to spend a little extra cash, you can still acquire many of these "gems." Four classic surface baits — well constructed and flawless in their action — that no topwater musky man should be without are: the Pflueger Globe, South Bend Surf-Oreno, Heddon Crazy Crawler, and the C.C. Roberts Mud Puppy. These lures are the "grandparents" of most modern day surface lures. Besides the Crazy Crawler, which goes for twice as much money, these lures can often be acquired for $12 to $20 at flea markets, garage sales, antique shops and bait swaps.

The Globe (the grandpappy of today's Chippewa, Slammer Topwater and Surf Roller) has long been a big fish producer. It works well in calm to choppy water and should be retrieved slowly and steadily, about the speed you would expect a mouse or chipmunk to swim. Too many anglers work a surface bait too fast, buzzing it across the surface. To maximize big fish production, I try to make the Globe appear to be a living thing swimming through the water — giving the lure an occasional, but ever so slight, twitch. This gives the lure just a hint of struggle.

The Globe can be made to produce two different sounds: 1.) By loosening the two screws that hold the prop onto the head and then backing off the prop an eighth-inch from the head, a rattling vibration will be created; 2.) By taking out those screws completely and, again, backing off the prop an eighth-inch from the head, the Globe will

The 'Grandparents' of Most Modern Day Surface Lures

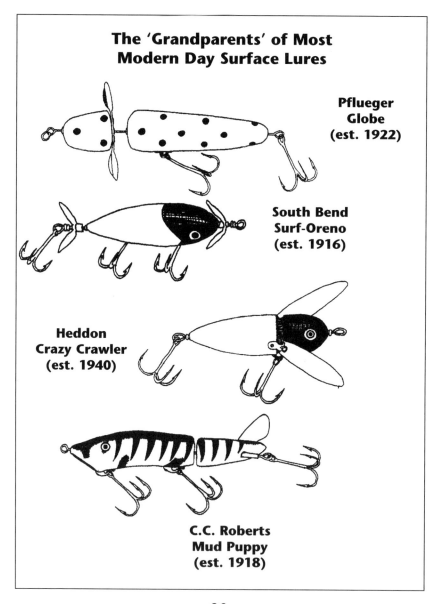

Pflueger
Globe
(est. 1922)

South Bend
Surf-Oreno
(est. 1916)

Heddon
Crazy Crawler
(est. 1940)

C.C. Roberts
Mud Puppy
(est. 1918)

make a more sloppy, "churgling" sound. (Slight modifications can be made to the Chippewa, Slammer and Surf Roller to yield similar results.)

The Surf-Oreno (the grandpappy of the old Bonnet and today's Cisco Kid Topper and Topper Stopper) also has racked up more than its share of trophy muskies over the years. The Surf-Oreno and Topper work well in calm water, a ripple, and a light chop and should be worked exactly as the Globe. They have props fore and aft which, if pitched in opposite directions, seem to make the lure track better. Occasionally, the back prop on a Topper won't spin; but if you experiment with both the degree of pitch and angle of prop bend, it will work.

John Dettloff's favorite fishing partner, his wife, Paulette Dettloff, with a 15-pounder she caught on a Globe.

Surface Bait Subtleties

The Cisco Kid Topper, recently reintroduced by Suick Manufacturing of Antigo, Wisconsin, has been around for some 40 years and has long had a reputation as a tried and true favorite. The Topper Stopper, one of the

Diehard musky man Pat Aaron with one of many nice muskies on the Bon-net lure. The bait was similar to the Surf-Oreno, with the exception that it had six treble hooks.

A week when the 40-pounders went wild. F. M. Packard holds his 40-pound 12-ounce fish from July 1956. This musky was caught on a Surf-Oreno.

newer members of the "Surf-Oreno family," can be worked slowly, but seems to produce best when worked at a bit faster pace so its larger props can stir up a louder and more frantic commotion.

The Crazy Crawler (younger "cousin" to the Jitterbug, older "brother" of the LeBoeuf Creeper, and grandpappy of today's Bauer Creeper and Creepin' Hogg and Hi-Fin's Creeper and Hawg Buster) is a more difficult lure to acquire but, having numerous 40-pound-plus musky catches to its credit, makes it worth finding. I must admit that, because these lures have given me some of the most explosive and heart stopping musky action of my life, the Creeper (or Crazy Crawler) is my all-time favorite musky lure.

Creepers are primarily used in quieter water but, if you can find one that will crawl well and maintain its sound in a light to moderate chop, use it! I like to use Creepers slowly — the same speed as a Globe or Topper — and with little variation. On occasion, when the Creeper is midway through the retrieve, I will briefly pick up the

Fluorescent orange lures like this Crazy Crawler are more visible to the muskies when the late summer algae blooms give the water a greenish tint.

speed of the lure for only a couple of cranks. This slight increase in speed is the type of subtle change that often triggers nearby muskies into striking.

The back-and-forth swimming or rocking motion of a Creeper somewhat resembles a duckling waddling across the water. And believe me, muskies do eat small ducks and ducklings. I can attest to this personally, after more than once seeing ducks get nailed by hungry muskies.

Tuning a Creeper is a difficult skill to master. It just takes practice. A Creeper's wings must be symmetrical in almost every sense to yield a balanced sound. I prefer the wings of a Creeper, when viewed from above, to extend outward from the head of the lure body at about an 80-degree angle. This will create the slower creep that I prefer. Decreasing the angle and bringing the wings in closer to the head of the lure, will create a faster, more frantic creep.

The entire top edge of each Creeper wing should be cupped forward more than the bottom edge of each wing is cupped. If the lure rolls over and spins around, increase the forward cup of the top edge of each wing until you have the maximum side-to-side rocking motion and the deepest pitched "plop-plop" sound. If the wings are cupped too far forward, you will lose some of the rocking action and the deeper sound that I prefer.

Surface Bait Subtleties

Wisconsin DNR legend Arthur Oehmcke with a nice Wisconsin musky taken on a Creeper.

The Mud Puppy (grandpappy of the Tally Wacker, Top Kick, Teasertail, and numerous other similar lures on the market today) is the oldest surface bait (1918) still available and in production today! This lure is preferred in

Lures

a calm to slight wave action. With its unique revolving tail piece, many old timers found it to better produce if the metal tail was cupped more to create a louder popping sound.

During the early 1980s, Hayward area guide Wayne Gutsch took the concept of the Mud Puppy and amplified it, creating a much noisier lure that worked well even into a moderate chop. The introduction of this lure, the Tally Wacker, marked the beginning of what was to become a long string of other Mud Puppy lure types to be made available.

Tuning these lures may be difficult at first, but again it just takes practice and close observation. As a rule, if you decrease the cup of the metal tail, you will increase the speed it revolves but you will get a quieter popping sound. If the cup is decreased even more, the popping sound will be completely eliminated and you will get a swishing, spinning sound. I prefer to increase the cup of the metal tail until it creates a louder, deeper popping sound — while still maintaining a pretty fast tail revolution.

The ideal speed to use these lures tends to be a bit faster than the speed a Globe or Topper is used. In some conditions, when the muskies are really aggressive, an even faster retrieve seems to work very well. However, when you work these Mud Puppy-type lures slower, they become more "Globe-like," creating a totally different action and still producing well — some anglers feel it has a better influence on big fish.

While most surface baits fit into the previously mentioned four families of surface lures, a few additional surface bait types remain. Through the years, there has been a varied assortment of Flaptail surface lure types available — ever since Heddon first introduced them in 1935. Attached to the rear end of these lures with a swivel is a metal flaptail that revolves around and splashes the water back and forth. Good fish-getters in their own right, Flaptails often are considered to be good "fish locators" because of the many blow ups and short hits they trigger.

Surface-jerkbaits like the old Zaragossa and the present day Giant Jackpot have a very unique topwater darting action that will often trigger action from muskies that normally won't hit another lure. To a degree, these lures also have "fish locator" reputations.

But I would be remiss to write about surface baits without mentioning one of the most revolutionary of all surface lures, unique in both its design and action — the Hawg Wobbler. It's like a "topwater Pikie Minnow" that makes a lot of noise! In fact — out of all the surface lures that I've listened to from under the water — the Hawg Wobbler creates the loudest vibration and can be heard farther away than any other lure. It makes several different kind of sounds — all at the same time.

When this lure first came out in 1978, it was so different that it didn't catch on right away. But, in short order, it was discovered to be a dynamite big fish bait. The Hawg Wobbler works best in quiet water conditions to a slight chop and should be retrieved slowly and steadily. All the lure's action is built in! The proper speed for a Hawg Wobbler is just fast enough so the lure has a nice easy wobbler and makes a good sound, while a very definite rhythmic vibration can be felt in your rod tip.

There's little tuning that needs to be done to a

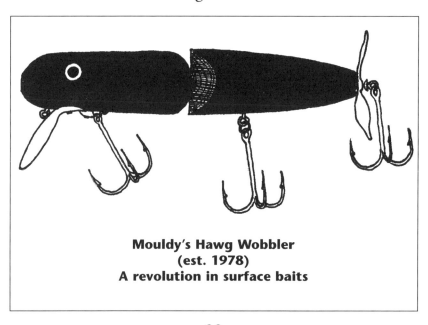

Mouldy's Hawg Wobbler
(est. 1978)
A revolution in surface baits

Surface Bait Subtleties

Hawg Wobbler. Most are ready to use when new. Some may need a minor lip bend to one side to offset a rolling over to the side problem that can occasionally occur. To strengthen and prolong the life of a Hawg Wobbler, put some waterproof epoxy on the threads of the two screw eyes that hold the front and back sections of the lure together.

Sharpening Hooks

How important are sharp hooks? Very! While it is true that a certain percentage of muskies "set themselves" and get hooked whether your hooks are sharp or not, if you rely only on catching the ones that "hit right," you're going to be losing many fish that you should be catching. If you're only catching one musky out of ten that hit, something may be wrong — it might be that your hooks aren't sharp enough. In order to maximize my percentage of boated muskies, I always adhere to the four following tips: Use razor sharp hooks, a very low stretch line, a fairly stiff rod, and a strong hookset. It works! Approximately half of the muskies that touch my lures — I catch.

There are three basic reasons for having dull hooks. First, many anglers have the misconception that new lures already have sharp hooks. Actually, in most cases, they are quite dull. If you could magnify the point of a new hook, you would see that the point is rounded or blunt. It must be sharpened so that the point tapers to a very needle sharp point. Some new hooks are sharper than others, but I haven't seen a new hook yet that couldn't at least use a little sharpening to make them ultra-sharp.

Secondly, many anglers sharpen their hooks improperly. There are several devices used to sharpen hooks — a grinder, a stone, one of many types of hook sharpeners now available, and a file. I prefer a file because, for me, it does the job best. You want to use a file that has some bite to it, one that has the ability to remove material easily when necessary.

My first step is to triangulate: sharpening three main sides of the point, always working the file toward the point of the hook. Only a couple of strokes are needed on each side so as not to oversharpen, in which you remove too much material. My second step is to lightly work all the way around the hook, going toward the point with the file, to finally give the hook a needle-like point. Angling the file too much will blunt the hook. I like to test my hook points by lightly touching them with my fingertips. Other people test hook sharpness by seeing if the point will grab onto their thumbnails.

And the third reason for having dull hooks is from just plain neglect. Many times it's the accomplished fisher-

Surface Bait Subtleties

men who are guilty of this. Many times I have noticed people who should know better who are using lures with dull hooks. Maybe it's easier for these veteran fishermen to neglect these kinds of things because they're not as hungry

Is it important to sharpen your hooks? You bet it is! Razor-sharp hooks paid off for John Dettloff with this 26 3/4-pounder that he caught on a Creeper on Aug. 28, 1981.

Sharpening Hooks

for muskies as they used to be. They let their guard down and get a little sloppy with the finer points of their sport and, not surprisingly, aren't catching as many muskies as they used to. Don't fall into this trap! Novice and expert musky hunters alike should make sure their hooks are sharp.

Two additional hook hints. Always have a hook sharpener in the boat — but keep it in a dry place so it won't rust. Also, always have a half a dozen pre-sharpened hooks on split rings handy, just in case you have to cut the hooks off a lure to release a musky and you still want to be able to use the same lure on your next spot. Just pop the new hooks on and you're in business.

Enticements

There are many types of enticements that trigger muskies into striking surface baits. First off, when fishing for active, shallow water muskies — fish that are relating to the surface — keep in mind that it is not uncommon for a musky to see your lure coming through the air, just before it hits the water. Some strikes will come simultaneously as your lure hits the water. So, be ready for it!

Remember — muskies' eyes are on the top of their heads and they look upward. They have been known to grab at low flying birds that skim the water for insects. I once had a musky dart out from underneath his haunt, come out of the water, and grab my Topper while it was still six inches above the water! If you fish long enough, you'll be amazed at what can happen.

The next, and one of the key enticements to be aware of, is the period of time just after your lure hits the water. The splash of your lure is often a big attractor to a feeding musky. And because the majority of strikes come just after the lure splashes down — and setting hooks with a surface lure tends to be more difficult — make sure you stop your reel spool with your thumb to take the bow out of your line just before your lure hits the water. With a tight line you'll have a strong hookset when those early strikes come.

Other key enticements that trigger many strikes are the subtle wrist action twitches or lure speed-ups that I only like to use sparingly during each cast. (Remember: one twitch will go a long way.) When I get a follow on a surface lure, I never like to stop my lure. The musky is

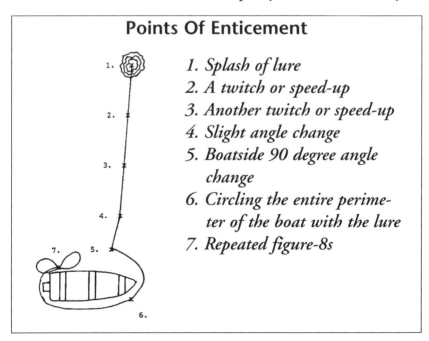

Points Of Enticement

1. *Splash of lure*
2. *A twitch or speed-up*
3. *Another twitch or speed-up*
4. *Slight angle change*
5. *Boatside 90 degree angle change*
6. *Circling the entire perimeter of the boat with the lure*
7. *Repeated figure-8s*

Surface Bait Subtleties

entranced on the lure's vibration (or sound) and, if the lure stops, so does the vibration. As far as the musky's concerned, the lure is gone and he may lose interest.

When I spot a follow behind a "prop bait" — a Globe or Topper, I'll continue to keep the lure coming its normal speed for a few feet. And if the musky doesn't strike, I'll try a very slight speed-up and then a light twitch. I keep repeating these steps until the lure gets near the boat.

But when I spot a follow behind a Creeper, Hawg Wobbler, or Mud Puppy-type lure (lures with much built-in action), there is little I can do to add further enticement so — aside from very slight occasional speed-ups — I'll just keep the lure coming at its regular speed. If the lure nears the boat but the musky still hasn't hit, don't rush it — you still have time to trigger a strike.

When the lure is about 10 feet away from the boat, I like to create a slight angle change by sweeping my rod tip off to one side. The resulting slight vector change of the lure often triggers strikes. If not, when the lure arrives boatside, make a 90-degree angle change. This irresistible enticement tricks many a finicky musky into hitting. It's a good idea to make sure you have your freespool button pressed and your thumb hard on the spool, just before you initiate this maneuver. This will enable you to get a good hookset, while at the same time allowing the musky to make its usually explosive first run — under the pressure of your thumb.

But, if the musky still doesn't hit on the right angle change, just continue pulling the lure alongside the boat, making sure the lure stays on the surface and maintains its normal speed. I'll slowly walk the lure around the entire perimeter of the boat, adding an occasional twitch here and there, as long as the musky keeps following. You could call it a huge "figure-zero" around the boat. Whether you choose to do a large figure-8 or make a huge oval next to the boat, or circle the entire boat with your lure, doesn't matter that much. What matters is that you do something that will keep your lure working near the boat for a prolonged period of time to entice boatside muskies into striking.

I once had a 43 1/2-inch musky follow an orange Topper (for the entire length of my cast) up to the boat, swim completely around the entire boat, and then hit the lure. Luckily I had my button pressed and thumb on the spool the whole time I was pulling my lure around the boat, because when the fish hit — it was very explosive! Had my reel been engaged with my tight drag, I could have lost my rod when the musky powered away.

Even if I don't notice a musky following my lure,

should I still do a figure-8 at the end of each cast? This is a question that I get asked by many of my guide clients. Well, without a doubt, a well executed figure-8 at the end of each cast is bound to increase your boatside catch percentage. But, realistically, it takes time to completely execute this maneuver after every single cast — time that will slightly impede the coverage of the area that you're fishing because of the resulting reduction in how many casts you will make into that area.

So in order to have the best of both worlds, at the end of each cast when using a surface bait, I always do an angle change next to the boat and then pull my lure parallel to the boat as far as I can reach — while carefully looking for the slightest hint of a musky behind my lure. If nothing is there, I'll quickly rifle out another cast in order to best cover the area. But if something doesn't look quite right or I even think I see any kind of a flash, I'll immediately break either into a figure-8 or will continue working the lure around the boat.

Never snatch the lure out of the water without at least doing an angle change next to the boat because you will eventually get burned and muff a good fish. And quite often it's the big fish, which tend to be a little lazier, that commonly come up late for your lure at the very last minute. You don't want to pull the lure away from these

Enticements

muskies — you want to catch them!

An "old musky man" from yesteryear, Walter J. Roman, demonstrates the proper speed of a surface lure — slow! A prime topwater evening ... cloudy with a slight ripple on the water.

When To Set?

This is a commonly asked question when it comes to surface baits. The simplistic answer is: to set on the feel, and not on the sound. But this is not as definitive an answer as it may seem.

The "feel" (any sort of contact that you can sense to be made with the lure) is the primary thing you should wait for before setting the hook. But don't always expect a hard "clobberjob" to tell you that a musky has hit. Many muskies will grab the lure and you won't feel anything more than a little nip or tick — sometimes picking it up as lightly as a panfish taking a jig. Or they'll grab the lure and will come toward the boat, creating slack line and a reduction in what you can feel. But both cases still represent lure contact and a "feel" that can be sensed by the angler. So, set the hook!

And don't ask me how, but some muskies can nail the lure without the angler detecting any "feel" at all. That's why you also have to watch your lure to detect some hits. So, even if you don't feel anything different, if your lure suddenly disappears or moves to the side, a musky probably has your lure and you should set! So be sure to use both your senses of feel and sight to detect surface bait strikes.

A brief comment on how I prefer to set my drag should be mentioned here. Since the majority of the muskies strike early in the retrieve, shortly after my lure hits the water, I choose to play the odds and have my drag set fairly tight to guarantee a solid hookset on the fish. My drag is set so it will pull out when it's under heavy pressure, though. Once my lure nears the boat, I prefer to press my freespool button and thumb the spool hard just before I begin working my lure boatside. This prepares me well for the boatside strikes.

Time of Year

On most waters, surface baits are very productive throughout the entire summer period — from early June through late September, when water temperatures are generally above 62 degrees. Now in the deeper, clear water lakes and in Canadian waters, where water temperatures warm more slowly, late June through early September tends to be the prime surface bait time.

Although it's primarily the wave action that determines which surface lure that I use, there are some seasonal factors that have influence on my lure selection.

Early in June, I like to lean toward using the smaller, quieter surface baits: such as the Surf-Oreno or Cisco Kid Topper.

Now, while Creepers and Mud Puppy-types (lures which, to me, both sound similar to a duckling scampering across the surface) are good throughout most of the season, they do seem to be at peak productivity after the ducklings hatch in late June or July. And these two lures seem to fade off a bit sooner than the Globe and Hawg

Wobbler — two of my favorite later season (mid September to early October) surface baits. During mid September — when jerkbaits really come into their own — don't neglect using surface-jerkbaits like the Giant

After this musky made two passes at John Dettloff's Globe, Richard Bartlett (left) caught and released this 45 1/2-incher on a Hawg Wobbler one-half hour later. This is a fine example of how the Hawg Wobbler can continue to be a good surface lure into fall.

Surface Bait Subtleties

Jackpot.

Once the water temperature drops below 62 degrees (usually in late September), the Hawg Wobbler seems to easily take the lead as my most productive late season surface bait. It's caught muskies for me as late as mid October and with water temperatures as low as 55 degrees. Without fail, from two hours before sundown till well after dark on

When this 18-pound class musky nailed John Dettloff's Globe in September, it proved that muskies will still hit surface baits during the midday and when it is rough and choppy. With Dettloff are Joe Jasek (left) and Jack Eiche (right).

56

Time of Year

those pleasant early fall evenings, a Hawg Wobbler will be one of my first lure choices. While that time of year (around turnover) can yield inconsistent action, there still seems to be a twilight shallow water musky movement that you can usually count on. This is inevitably the season's last hurrah for surface lures.

The Bewitching Hour, And After

Just in case you haven't heard of the term, "the bewitching hour," applied to musky fishing, it refers to that hour or so long period that starts when the sun begins to touch the treeline and lasts until well past dark. This is prime time on many waters; one of the most consistent musky feeding periods of the day.

Unfortunately, many anglers miss out on the great fishing this time period offers because, by dusk, they head back to camp and call it a day. Tired, afraid of getting lost on an unfamiliar body of water, or chased in by the legions of hungry mosquitoes that usually come out at dusk, these fishermen drastically decrease their odds of catching a musky by quitting too soon.

It is during these low light hours of the evening that the waters of the northwoods generally calm down to provide musky hunters with just the perfect conditions to use surface baits. Throughout the years, this time period has provided me with just the right "window of opportunity" to boat many a musky. In fact, even on the days when my resort duties have kept me too busy to get on the water, I have always tried my best to sneak out for a quick 15-minute "fix" of musky fishing around dusk. I remember one such evening well:

It was on August 18, 1984. A busy work day at the resort had successfully kept me off the water — at least until I noticed the sun beginning to set. Then my pulse began to quicken and I became itchy to hit just one close by spot. But it was a quarter to 9 — and I had bar duty that night beginning at 9! So, while the going was still good, I grabbed my rod — which happened to have an orange Topper hooked onto it — and made a beeline for my boat.

I asked a teenager named Rick, who happened to be standing on the dock, if he wanted to go for a 15-minute boat ride. So into my boat he jumped and we were off to the Church Bars, one of the Chippewa Flowage's many renowned areas. Within two minutes I was casting toward a favorite weedbed of mine and, even though I only had time for about 10 casts, I felt confident. For this was "the bewitching hour" and I was on some mighty good water!

After explaining to Rick what to do if I tied into a musky, he just laughed with disbelief at the prospect of me catching a musky on such short notice. But on my very next cast, something nailed my Topper just as I began my retrieve! Rick was looking the other way at the time and didn't believe me when I frantically yelled, "I got one!" — until he saw my rod doubled over and a fine specimen of a musky come headshaking out of the water and go airborne.

"Oh my God! It's a 40-pounder!" Rick shouted. I told him it was big, but not that big. "It's probably a 25-pounder," I said.

The musky made a hard run that couldn't be stopped, right through a big weedbed. I thought I would lose him for sure after he got tangled in the weeds but, after putting enough pressure on him to pump him out of the weedbed, the musky reacted by soaring back into the air. Weeds flew in all directions!

This fish fought hard, circling the boat at least six times and making two more wild leaps. The musky was hyped up — and so were we! With Rick's assistance, I was able to get the musky into my net when the time was right. After unhooking and measuring it, I had planned on releasing it but it had literally "fought its heart out" and wouldn't revive. So I brought it in — and just in the nick of time to open up our bar.

The musky, 45 inches long and just over 24 pounds,

attracted an immediate crowd back at the resort. A couple of the guests wondered where I had gotten that big fish from, knowing that I was too busy to fish that day. Pointing right across the lake, I said, "Right over there.

The 45-inch, 24-pound musky caught by John Dettloff by fishing for only 10 minutes — during just the right "window of opportunity" afforded by the bewitching hour.

Surface Bait Subtleties

The timing happened to be just right, after all ... it's the bewitching hour."

I can remember another August evening when I should have been home working, but did manage to sneak out for a little evening musky fishing. As it turned out, that day (August 22, 1989) stands as one of the most memorable musky fishing days of my life.

I was in the middle of a roofing project on my house that day and, once I realized that sundown was only an hour away, thoughts of musky fishing quickly entered my mind. I was hoping to finish my project that night, but the excitement of catching a nice 38 1/2-inch musky on a Globe that morning only served to make me crave even more action. And the light north breeze that was rippling the water on that clear evening was just too much for me to withstand. For this signaled the leading edge of a cold front — a big fish circumstance that should never be ignored!

No longer desiring to pound nails, I soon found myself pounding the water in the Church Bars vicinity. As soon as I got out there I caught an undersized musky on one of those "hairy things" — I think it's called a bucktail! (Yes, I use lures other than surface baits on occasion. A productive fisherman must be versatile.) I then moved to a nearby spot and switched to my big black Globe, expecting something much bigger to hit. And, after only a few minutes, I caught another musky, but it was only 18 inches long! A cute little guy, though.

As the sun finally began to fully disappear from sight, I quickly advanced to another nearby "guaranteed big fish spot." I was pulling out all the stops, switching to one of my favorite lures, a black Creeper, with very high hopes. On my first cast a musky waked and surfaced behind my lure, finally nailing it hard right next to the boat. An enjoyable little tussle ensued; but the culprit that ended up almost mortally destroying my Creeper turned out to be another undersized fish — 29 1/2 inches long.

After fishing out the rest of that spot, I realized I only had time to zip over to one more place — a small bar that had produced a good 20-pound-plus musky for me, late at night, just 10 days earlier. Upon readjusting my Creeper and sharpening a few hooks, I was again in business. Even though it was dusk — and getting darker by the minute — I neglected to put on my headlamp for fear that I would miss out on a cast. When you're on a good spot and it's prime time, it's difficult to put down your rod even for a minute!

It was a peaceful evening with no other boats in sight. Working around the entire bar, I cast my Creeper over the the shallow cabbage weeds. It was around 9 p.m.

when a musky hit way out. I set the hook and felt the familiar headshaking that is unique to a musky. Seemingly stuck in a temporary small fish jag, I was hoping for just a legal-sized fish. And the fact that this was my fifth musky catch for the day made me calmer than usual.

Not having my headlight on made it more difficult for me to see just how big a fish I had on — until I got the musky on the west side of the boat where there was just enough light to see the broad back of a big(!) fish. Then I got excited!

The musky fought fairly close to the boat, making three short runs away from me. And as it authoritatively circled the boat, it displayed the power that could only belong to a 30-pounder. I was sure I had hold of a "wall-hanger." After working the fish back around to the lighter side of the boat, I was able to get it into my net on my second attempt. I wasn't sure exactly how big the fish was; all I could see was the silhouette of a huge head staring back at me.

While I fumbled to finally put on my headlight, the musky once again showed off his brute power by diving deep into my net bag — ripping it right out of my hands and pulling it toward the bottom. My rod, which was still hooked onto the fish, even began to go overboard! Quickly reaching down and grabbing the rim of my net, I was able

The Bewitching Hour, And After

The 30-pounder that nailed John Dettloff's Creeper after dark during late August 1989 was cause for a celebration! Dettloff caught five muskies that day, four of which fell to surface baits.

to regain the upper hand on this musky. And after picking the musky out of my net and measuring it, I figured it should go around 30 pounds. This satisfied the personal size limit I had set for myself at that time, so I proudly went roaring in with my catch. The musky ended up tipping the scales at 30 pounds 1 ounce.

Many anglers don't realize that, by the time total darkness sets in, practically all the mosquitoes are gone and it is very comfortable to fish. While dusk and first dark (the bewitching hour) can be considered prime time, it should be realized that — during the summertime — musky fishing continues to be great well into the night and into the wee hours of the morning as well.

After fishing round the clock on many occasions over the years, I have noticed somewhat of a slow down in musky action after 1 a.m. Of course, I must admit, that I'm not able to fish on a regular basis after that late hour. A person does have to sleep sometime! But I have made more than my share of midnight musky runs over the years and it seems that the period around 12:30 a.m. to 1 a.m. provides me with the latest consistent good musky fishing action. Believe me, big fish can still be found moving around at that late hour!

I can remember closing up our tavern early one night and instigating one such midnight excursion about

The Bewitching Hour, And After

10 years ago. Fellow musky fishing maniacs, Al Denninger and Charlie Thompson, joined me that night — a night that none of us will ever forget! We each were using Globes, covering every possible corner of a large shallow sand bar that we were slowly drifting. It was pitch dark in all directions and the only clue we had as to where we were was that we could still see my resort's light looming in the distance.

Near the end of our drift, I experienced a short hit behind my Globe that was so incredibly loud and explosive that it caused all three of us to immediately set our hooks! The fish never actually touched my lure, so the next thing we knew, three big Globes came hurling toward my boat at hazardous velocities. It's a hard call to make when deciding on whether to set on those kind of hits. I couldn't begin to guess how big that musky was — it had to be 30-pound class or better. Denninger said that it sounded like someone had dropped a pick-up truck out of the sky and into the water behind my lure!

I have devoted a fair amount of attention to night fishing for muskies in this section for one simple reason because to me, it largely typifies what musky fishing is all about. Night fishing for muskies takes all of the well-known virtues of musky fishing and magnifies them ... tenfold! No other aspect of musky fishing is so full of

The savage fury of this 41-inch musky is displayed as the guide nets his client's nice catch. This fish was tricked by a Hawg Wobbler.

unbridled thrills and excitement and induces such intense anticipation and fright, while at the same time taking place during one of the most peaceful and solitary times of the entire day. In short, it's what I look forward to more than any other part of musky fishing.

A couple of final comments about night fishing: Don't be surprised to catch an occasional big walleye after dark while musky fishing. At night time, big walleyes often frequent the same territory as muskies. And, although it's primarily surface baits that I'm throwing after dark, I won't hesitate to throw a bucktail if it's choppy. During such conditions bucktails can be more effective. Just because a bucktail doesn't make any noise that you can hear, believe me — they make a vibration underwater that the muskies can sense equally well in most cases.

The author's wife, Paulette Dettloff, with a "surface bait bonus" — a beautiful 29-inch walleye that she caught on a black Globe.

Moon Phases

Many people believe that the phases of the moon affect the behavior of people, animals, and yes, even fish. The full moon has especially held fascination, and even horror, for many people since the earliest of times. Old folklore is full of stories about werewolves appearing at the time of the full moon. Well, I haven't seen any werewolves but I have seen some monster muskies right after the full moon! Trophy muskies do seem to be more active during certain phases of the moon.

There have been many articles published discussing the relationship between the phases of the moon and big musky activity. After sifting through my vast collection of big fish data from my favorite body of water, the Chippewa Flowage, I have several moon phase observations to share. Although these observations come from one specific body of water, a dark water flowage (reservoir), I have no reason to believe that the following trends won't be found to be true in other types of waters as well.

Having exact catch dates for 319 different catches over 30 pounds (covering over a 70-year period), gives me an excellent opportunity to see how the phases of the moon have related to the catching of these big muskies. It takes approximately 29 days for the moon to revolve around the earth, going from full moon back to full moon. This time duration is known as the lunar month and can be divided into 30 lunar days (for simplicity) on a graph. Day 2 is the day of the last quarter, Day 10 is the day of the new moon, Day 18 is the day of the first quarter, and Day 25 is the day of the full moon on the graph. The number of 30-pound muskies caught during each lunar day can be plotted on the graph to see if any patterns are evident. Since 319 muskies catches can be plotted onto this 30-day graph, an average lunar day would be considered about 10 fish. Anything exceeding 10 fish caught during a given lunar day could be considered an above average 30-pound musky day.

There seem to be two noticeable peak periods for 30-pound plus musky catches during the lunar month. First, the five-day period after the new moon is the longest lasting peak period, with 76 out of the 319 (or 24 percent) big muskies being caught during this rela-

Surface Bait Subtleties

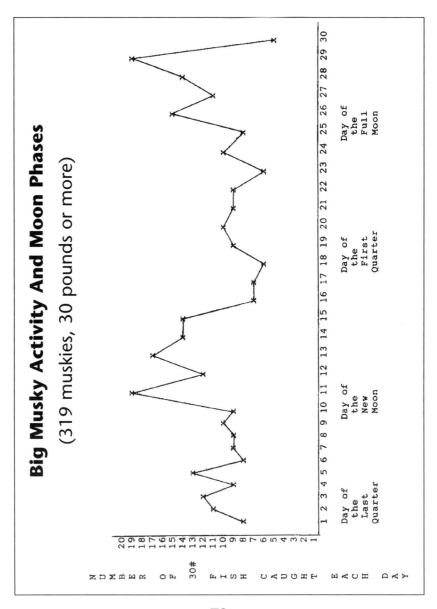

72

tively short time frame. And secondly, the four-day period after the full moon is also a highly productive big fish period, with 59 out of the 319 (or 18 1/2 percent) big muskies being caught during this time frame. The day after the new moon (Day 11) and the fourth day after the full moon (Day 29) are, statistically, the best two 30-pound musky days of the lunar month — where the odds of catching a big fish are double what they are on the average day.

These peak moon phase periods, in the long run, tend to be a little more productive for trophy-sized muskies. But that is not to say that a big musky can't be taken during a below average lunar day. Big muskies have been caught all throughout the lunar month. If you decide not to fish just because it's a below average day, you could miss out on catching a trophy of a lifetime. Remember, the weather conditions can easily override the effects of the moon phases and dictate more than any other single factor whether you're going to catch fish.

I have noticed that, as a rule, night fishing for muskies during a bright full moon is not very productive. Fishing will still be good in the evening and even while the moon is rising, but once the moon rises high enough to become bright in the sky, there seems to be little musky activity. But if it happens to be cloudy or overcast enough to conceal the bright full moon, then the nighttime musky fishing will usually remain good. So it seems that the bright light of the moon does something to turn the muskies off. And on the nights when the full moon is first rising, I'll try to fish the shadowy sides of islands and shorelines that are protected from the direct light of the moon. This gives me a little extra time to hit a few more spots before the moon gets too high in the sky and slows things down.

Two years ago, during the August full moon, I found myself fishing an island one night until well after the moon had risen. It had gotten to the point where it became bright enough that I figured my chances at some action were just about over. But it was a beautiful and serene night to be out on the water, so I was in no particular hurry to go in. Besides, I was about to come up to the shadowy side of the island!

The trees on the west side of the island created a dark little sanctuary, to which I excitedly threw my black Heddon Crazy Crawler. On what was to be my last cast, a musky hit short behind the lure — making a very impressive, deep sounding, explosion. As soon as I got my lure in, I quickly shot another cast right into the same exact spot and — the second my lure touched the water this big musky nailed it hard! The resulting battle

Moon Phases

The author briefly holds a 25-pound class musky up for a photo before releasing it. The fish hit a Crazy Crawler on the shaded side of an island during a bright full moon in August of 1993.

that this wild 45 1/2-inch musky gave me, got me so wound up that I could hardly sleep that night! So after the full moon rises — fish the shadows!

One secret that I've learned that compensates me for the ease up in night action during the full moon, is that the early morning hours are very productive during this period. Because the muskies hardly feed at all during the night, it seems as if they are extra hungry once morning comes.

I freely admit that I'm a night owl who hates to wake up early in the morning, but during the full moon period, I will still make it a point to get out on the water at daybreak whenever possible. This is a key time period that has repeatedly shown me many big muskies!

Weather Conditions & Lure Selection

While the low light hours of the morning and evening tend to be the prime surface bait hours, topwater lures can produce well all day long. More than the time of day, it's the factors of wave action, sky conditions, water clarity/turbidity, and water temperature that determine whether I'll throw a surface bait.

Heavy winds, "mile high" clear blue skies, very clear water, and uncomfortably high water temperatures in the upper 70s all contribute to making surface bait fishing less productive. However, when the wave action is slight to moderate, sky conditions are mostly cloudy to overcast, the water is stained, murky, or has an algae bloom, and water temperatures are in the upper 60s to lower 70s —

these factors (either individually or, better yet, in combination) make for some very effective surface bait fishing, regardless of the time of day. The key is: when the weather conditions are conducive for bringing the muskies shallower or closer to the surface, don't be afraid to use surface lures!

Talk about weather conditions — leaden skies and a slight chop on the water! Here Chippewa Flowage legend Bruce Tasker maneuvers his boat near a Chip hotspot. Tasker started musky fishing around 1930.

Fishing Deep Water With Surface Baits

Many anglers think about surface bait fishing as just a shallow water method, primarily to be used in three to six feet of water. But topwater lures are much more versatile than that, being productive at a wide variety of depth ranges. It may sound a little radical to use surface baits over deeper water, but it works!

Generally, the depth at which the outer edge of the weedline grows in a given body of water is the target depth that an angler should try to work. In the darker water lakes and flowages that depth range is shallow (from five to 10 feet), but on the clearer, natural lakes or on many Canadian shield lakes that depth range is deeper (from 14 to 20 feet). And it is on the deeper weedlines of these clearer waters that using surface lures is often an overlooked method.

Surface baits usually throw more vibration than other types of lures and have surprising "calling power." A musky can be induced to come a long way for a surface bait especially in the clearer lakes where they can see much farther. If the fish are there, in the deep weeds, during the right conditions a surface bait can be highly effective.

Another type of deep structure that is overlooked by surface bait users is the deeper stump clusters that can be found in reservoirs and flowages. A bucktail or jerkbait is usually a musky hunter's first choice when fishing deep wood in seven to 14 feet of water and, in many cases, that would be the more productive lure presentation to use — but not always. If the proper weather or low light conditions are occurring, it's likely the muskies will be suspending above the deep wood — whether it be stumps, brush, or even cribs. This is an opportune occasion to use a surface lure, even though the water may be as deep as seven to 14 feet.

Another circumstance that can produce some good deep water surface bait action is when the muskies suspend in deeper water, not very far below the surface, just off of the shallower structures — whether it be a weedline or edge of a shallow bar. It is common during the mid summer period — especially when a storm is brewing — to find muskies suspending over deeper water (12 to 25 feet), but still relating to the surface. Also, during this modern age of high speed bass boats frequently thundering over the shallower traditional musky bars, it's more likely that some muskies will spook out of the shallows and move to the deeper water.

But you don't want to spend all of your time fishing

Targeting "deep water" on a Canadian shield lake where the weedline ends at 14 to 20 feet can be highly productive. John Benson caught this 47 1/2-inch musky in 1991 from Lake of the Woods on a Water Thumper.

Fishing Deep Water With Surface Baits

just for those suspended muskies. Because, by and large, your most consistent success will still be on the structure itself, in the weeds or on the bar. It's just that it's worthwhile to start and finish deep while you are fishing the traditional shallower structures. Get into the habit of occasionally throwing out toward the deeper water while you are casting the shallower high percentage areas and you may be surprised to see just how effectively your surface lures will work on those suspended muskies — and many times they will be the bigger fish!

I learned this lesson early on in my musky fishing career after tangling with one of the biggest muskies I've ever seen. I hooked it on a Globe fished over about 14 feet of water. And even though this occurred nearly 18 years ago, it remains as one of the most vivid and haunting musky experiences of my life:

It was back on July 27, 1977, when I chose to embark on a serious big fish quest, planning to spend my entire evening on Pete's and Fleming's bars — two of the Chippewa Flowage's best-known big fish spots. There was a heavy overcast sky and a southwest wind; conditions were perfect. It was the kind of a night where I was on pins and needles on every cast, expecting something really big to hit at any moment. After making several drifts across Big Pete's Bar, I noticed the waters begin to calm and the western sky darken with a severe storm threatening to push its way in. So I quickly moved to Fleming's Bar, where I heard a 40-pounder had been active.

There used to be four tall stumps near the edge of the old river bed on the southeast corner of the bar. I figured I'd start out deep and gradually work my way toward those four stumps. By then, thunder was rumbling, lightning was filling the sky in the distance, and the water became as calm as glass. It was getting darker by the minute and it wasn't even 8 p.m. yet. This was the calm before the storm! The surface of the water was as black as I've ever seen it and my krackle Globe pushed up an eerily contrastive, white wake.

Not quite up to the four stumps and the edge of the bar, I must have cast into about 14 feet of water when I got a tremendous hit. I noticed the huge head of a musky, seemingly in slow motion, come up behind my Globe and engulf it, turning off to one side and giving me a good glimpse of its big thick body. And even today, after 21 years of musky fishing, I can state without reservation that it was the biggest head of a musky that I have ever seen. It's open mouth resembled a small pail!

Upon seeing this sight, even though I was propelled into an immediate state of fright, I still was able to automatically set the hooks ... setting with so much power that

Fishing Deep Water With Surface Baits

I straightened the big musky's head back out to where it was again facing straight at me. The musky reacted by pulling back so hard and turning its head back off to the side, that it completely straightened out both my arms. "This fish is too big!" I thought.

After showing its tail, which was a pretty impressive distance behind the musky's head, it submerged into the black depths and slowly made its way toward my boat. It stopped a couple of times and just "hung" in the water and wouldn't move. Upon pumping my rod to get the musky moving again, the fish soon ended up right underneath my boat — but about 10 feet below the surface. The fish just lay there motionless and felt like dead weight on the end of my rod.

Not knowing what to do next, I slowly began to pump the fish up toward the surface. As I was bringing the fish upward I could feel an occasional slow, powerful head-shake from the musky.

My anticipation was incredibly high as I was just about to raise the fish to the surface, but — just before that — the huge musky just opened up its mouth and the Globe floated to the surface. The fish was gone, vanishing like a phantom! Evidently, the musky never had been hooked and was just clamped onto the lure with its powerful jaws.

Surface Bait Subtleties

After getting such a good look at this musky, I have absolutely no doubt that it was easily over 40 pounds and maybe could have been in the mid 40-pound range. The big storm which had been threatening had skittered around and didn't quite hit where I was. But the thunder still rumbled, reminding me that the conditions for musky fishing were still prime. I half-heartedly picked up my rod to cast again but, because the experience with this huge fish was so intense (and I was probably in a mild state of shock), I discovered that all of the strength in my hands was gone and I couldn't even grip my rod. In fact for the next three weeks my hands were so affected that I could only fish for short durations of time before my hands would again lose their grip.

This experience taught me the hard way the importance of using a stiff rod with enough backbone to provide a good hookset, and a low-stretch braided line. For I happened to be using a longer, whippy rod and monofilament line — a grave mistake when using large wooden plugs. Now, maybe I still wouldn't have caught that huge musky if I had had heavier tackle; but if I would have been using a more powerful rod and my Cortland Micron 40-pound test braided line, I know my chances of hooking and landing that fish would have been much higher!

Lure Color

There has yet to have been anything mentioned about lure color because I consider it secondary to everything stated up until this point. That is not to say that lure color should be discounted; it's just not as critical as the action (or sound) of the lure. There's an old Chippewa Flowage saying about choosing the best color for a surface bait: "Any color is good, as long as it is black!"

Black is a very basic but consistently productive lure color that shouldn't be overlooked. It works! Perhaps in the darker waters like the flowage, black is so effective because it casts a better — more visible — silhouette against the lighter sky in the background.

I have noticed that greenish lures have been consistently "hot" on the Chippewa Flowage — where crappies happen to make up a big part of the muskies' diet. This helps to support the "match the hatch" concept. Another very productive color scheme that further bolsters this sage guideline is a mottled black and gold or black and yellow pattern. Where walleyes are an abundant forage fish, this color pattern is one of my favorites. And when the water has a greenish tint or a heavy algae bloom, I prefer fluorescent orange because it is more visible.

So while it's primarily the sound of your surface lure that draws in the muskies, having a lure color that both matches the hatch and is more easily visible is bound to — especially during specific circumstances — put more muskies into your boat!

Lure Maintenance

As time goes by and your favorite surface baits become riddled with tooth marks, you run the risk of your wooden lures becoming waterlogged. If that happens, you will notice that much of the sound of these lures will be lost. To remedy this situation, hang the lure in a very hot, dry place, like from a rafter in your attic. Let it hang and dry out for several days and then brush on a good coating of rod spar varnish or gun stock varnish. This will seal the lure and restore the sound it once had.

Putting These Tips Into Practice

W hat follows are some additional musky fishing accounts that further illustrate the importance of a cross section of the finer points of surface bait fishing for muskies:

I've heard the question, "Yeah, but will really big muskies hit surface baits?" enough times that it certainly deserves an answer. Yes, even the "super fish" — muskies that are in the 50-pound class and beyond — will indeed grab a surface lure. During the early 1950s, a world record class musky was lost by two different individuals, both using surface baits, on Cranberry Bar on the Chippewa Flowage.

Pioneer flowage guide Harry Lessard was guiding Carl Feldtkeller (around 1951) on the East Cranberry Bar when they tied into the monster on a Frog LeBoeuf Creeper, a lure which had been introduced just a few years earlier. The fish hit, making one tremendous boil, and came right toward the boat. When it passed by the boat, both men got such a good look at the fish that they knew they had hold of a possible world record class fish. During his lifetime's worth of musky fishing, it was definitely the biggest musky that Lessard had ever seen.

After the fish passed on by and headed away from the boat, Harry hollered to Carl to let the musky take some line and get out a ways — and then set the hook. But when Carl braced his hand on the reel handle to try to stop the fish and set the hook, Harry remembered that all he could hear was the grinding of gears. There was no star drag on the Pflueger Supreme reel that Carl was using. With the gears of the reel stripped and the reel not functioning properly, the musky took out as much line as it wanted and then broke off.

This particular musky must have had an appetite for surface baits because the next season, on the Labor Day weekend of 1952, three other flowage fishermen had an encounter with, most likely, the same monster musky — this time on a frog-colored Bon-net. In the same area where Lessard's client had lost the big one, John Kondrasuk (accompanied by guides Bruce Tasker and John

Surface Bait Subtleties

Zeug) tangled with that fish. The three men, all very experienced musky hunters, got a good look at the length of the fish, figuring it would go about six feet in length and would have been a world record if caught! The musky eventually hung the Bon-net up in a stump, tearing two gang hooks right off the lure!

Another big fish story that had a happier ending was

the story of how young Fritz Ackley — who later became a professional baseball player for 13 years for the Chicago White Sox, St. Louis Cardinals, and Pittsburgh Pirates — caught a near 50-pound musky on a red-headed Pflueger Globe when he was only 15 years old. This is the story, in his own words, of the catching of his Chippewa Flowage prize, back on June 27, 1952:

"Eddie Bergdahl, a friend who had never before fished for muskies,

Art Kelsey Sr. caught this 54-pound, 55-inch musky on a Globe in the late 1930s — further proof that monsters like surface baits.

94

Putting These Tips Into Practice

and I decided to go out fishing. He was about to be in for quite an initiation! My father was a guide and wasn't working that day, so we had his boat to use along with the pick of some very good equipment. We started out from Clement's Deerfoot Lodge and headed right over to Pete's Bar. Right on the shallow part of the bar, but near the dropoff, I had a big musky follow my Creeper to the boat. We tried and tried but couldn't get it back up again. So we came back the next day.

"It was overcast with a nice ripple — a good musky day. It was about 5 p.m. and, within just a matter of minutes, the musky hit my Globe, showing us just how huge he really was! Early on in the fight, I brought the musky boatside and Eddie shot at it with the pistol — but missed. The fish tore out of there like you wouldn't believe, pert' near running all of the line off my Pflueger reel. The musky fought like crazy, taking total control of the situation.

"While all this was transpiring, Eddie just sat there spellbound, unable to help me in any way. He couldn't even row the boat for me. Luckily, between the breeze blowing the right way and the musky pulling our boat, we ended up in the deeper water off the bar — free from any snags or obstructions. The musky broke water several more times and each time he made a long run I had to snub him, to turn him before he would run me out of line. After 15 minutes of this tiring tug-o-war, I finally got the musky back into shooting range.

"Since the pistol didn't get him the first time around, I decided to use the .32 Special deer rifle that I happened to have along. As Eddie quickly loaded a shell into the rifle, I told him, 'Give me the gun, I'll shoot it!' Once the musky was up on the surface, about 20 feet away,

Eddie Bergdahl (left) and Fritz Ackley (right) with Ackley's 49 3/4-pound, 55-inch trophy from June 1952.

Putting These Tips Into Practice

I took aim right over the top of its back and shot — only grazing and temporarily stunning the fish. I then worked the musky to the boat, gaffed him, and hauled it aboard.

"I can remember tying a rope through the musky's gills, out its huge mouth, and into a slip knot — tying the other end of it around my leg. If he was going back into the water, I was going to go in with him! And it's a good thing I had the musky tied up too because, being only knocked out from the shot, the musky came back to and started going wild in the boat. We finally subdued him by clubbing him. The fish weighed in at 49 3/4 pounds and was 55 inches long."

In case you're wondering if there have been any recent sightings of a possible record class musky, the answer is yes — only four years ago one was lost on the flowage. But since it was lost on a bucktail, I chose not to elaborate on it. We'll save that one for a future bucktail book!

But I can remember very well when, not too long ago, Jim Burns, a good friend of mine, came in from fishing with a look on his face similar to that of the one that Moses had when he first came down from Mt. Sinai — he was as pale as a ghost! The circumstances pertaining to the record class musky that Jim had on and lost on an orange Topper also apply to the next fine point of surface bait

Surface Bait Subtleties

fishing: do not neglect your surface baits in the rougher water! When it's really windy and your boat is rapidly being pushed through an area, using a fast retrieval lure like a bucktail will give you the best coverage of the area because you will be able to get more casts out. But, if it's rough and the waves are rolling more, and your boat really isn't being carried along that quickly, then it's not as critical to use a fast retrieval lure and certain surface baits will still produce very well. It was during these kind of rough, rolling waves that Jim Burns tied into his potential record breaker on a mid August morning in 1975:

A southerly wind, building up some good-sized waves on Pete's Bar, was slowly pushing Burns' boat along, right across the top of the bar. He slowly worked his home-made, slightly oversized, orange Topper through the swells. Partway through his drift, he noticed the head of a huge musky snatch his lure off of one of the waves. And it had length that just wouldn't quit! Jim figured it had to be a record class fish.

Jim set the hook but, because the wind was pushing his boat toward the fish, he had trouble keeping a tight line to the fish. The huge musky just lay on the surface shaking its head back and forth, eventually throwing the Topper. The musky remained on the surface just long enough to deeply implant its image permanently in Jim's memory and then ... sank away and vanished!

Is it worth throwing surface lures early in the season? While smaller-sized bucktails and Rapalas are my first lure choices for musky fishing during the early season, surface baits will produce in the spring if the conditions are right. Again, it's the weather that is the biggest determiner as to how the fish will bite and what methods will be most productive. Many of the early season muskies that I raise will often hit short on surface lures but, if a prolonged stretch of warm weather is able to warm up the shallows and make the muskies a bit more aggressive, surface baits can produce.

I remember fishing a favorite early season shoreline near Cranberry Bar during the last week of May in 1978 when I had a dandy follow a Globe right up to the boat. After throwing my standard assortment of springtime lures to no avail, I told my companion, Tony Bartlett, "I don't care what time of year it is, I'm going to throw my killer black and yellow Globe! And on my very first cast, into about seven feet of water, I noticed a light colored shadow behind my lure. I whispered to Tony to look and both of our eyes bugged out as a fat, obviously eggbound, near 50-inch musky followed my Globe right up to the boat and just lay there for a full minute before sinking away. This fish wasn't in the mood to eat — it was there to spawn —

but the Globe still captured its interest. This fish wasn't far from being 40 pounds!

And on Memorial Day weekend, 21 years earlier (in 1957), it was a surface lure that nailed a 53-inch,

Bunny Gage (left) and Jerry Marcin with their 38-pound 53-inch Chippewa Flowage musky caught on a Musk-E-Munk in May 1957.

Putting These Tips Into Practice

38-pound beauty for "Bunny" Gage off of Cranberry Bar. He was casting a black and white Marathon Musk-E-Munk (or "Shaving Brush" as the old-timers referred to it) into the shallow water near the corner of a small bulrush island. As soon as the lure hit the water, BAM! — the musky hit and came at the boat turning and rolling on the surface. Bunny was reeling in as fast as he could trying to keep up with the fish. Because the water was a few feet down at that time, there were exposed stumps all over that area. Bunny's partner, Jerry Marcin, who was on the oars, manipulated the boat out of the stumps toward the deeper water — banging into several stumps along the way. Upon reaching the deeper water, Marcin was finally able to subdue the musky by shooting it. Don't try to tell these men that surface baits don't work in May!

It's sucker time, time to put away your surface lures ... right? Wrong! Just because suckers begin to produce some fish in mid to late September doesn't mean it's time to quit using surface lures. Granted, during those first serious cold fronts that occur at that time, you're better off using a bucktail, jerkbait, or even a sucker; but — right up until mid October — topwater lures can still produce very well. As long as you can get some warmer weather or are fishing around dawn or dusk, surface baits (especially the Hawg Wobbler) can still "do some damage" during the early fall.

I remember one late September four years ago (1991) when, after a great spree of topwater action during the month of September, a major cold snap had brought a halt to my surface bait action. All of a sudden suckers were working.

After an evening of sucker fishing didn't yield anything for me, calmer conditions and an ever so slight warmup had me attach my gold Hawg Wobbler back on my casting rod. By the time it had become pitch dark I found myself casting Fleming's Bar with a good measure of confidence. It was still pretty nippy, and my hands were just a bit numb, but I knew the muskies still could be found shallow at this time of year once it became dusk. And sure enough, by the time the night was over, I had a nice 24-pound class musky in the boat. A quick release had the musky soon on its way back to its home turf.

Another one of many cases where the Hawg Wobbler came through during the fall period was on September 28, 1980, for my dad, Ron Dettloff. The entire month of September of that year was quite warm, making for consistent surface bait fishing right through early October. After getting fired up by a 37 1/2-pound beauty that Wayne Gutsch had guided one of our resort guests to that morning, my dad took his companion, John Carbine, out that evening to get in on some of this great fishing.

At around 6 p.m., my dad caught a 30-pounder on his black Hawg Wobbler, casting shallow — near a gravelly point. He was just slowly chugging his lure along when the musky nailed it on the very first cast he made into that spot. Luckily, he had just retied his knot before catching that musky. The fish was really hyped up, making two long powerful runs that strained my dad's tackle to the limit.

Once they got the fish into the net, it went wild in the bag and exploded the plastic yoke of the net. The two men had to think fast, hauling the fish into the boat by grabbing the rim of the net. Lesson: never lift a big fish into the boat using only the handle of the net! Grab near the yoke of the net with one hand and the rim of the net with your other hand, when preparing to haul a heavy fish into the boat.

Remember, never allow slack line to occur when your lure first hits the water. To guarantee a positive hook-set on those fish that nail your lure just after it impacts the water, make sure that you have a tight line to your lure as it is hitting the water. One experience that most vividly drives this point home occurred to me back in 1985, on the fifth of July:

I had taken one of our resort guests out on one of his first musky fishing outings. Once the "bewitching hour" was upon us, I sneaked in on a favorite small weed point of mine near the Cranberry Narrows. Believing in being as quiet as possible when approaching a spot so as not to spook the fish, I shut the motor off far from the key weedbed I wanted to fish. Quietly working my way toward that weedbed, we soon were in position.

Shooting a long cast with my orange Topper to the weedbed, I noticed a hole (six feet in diameter!) open up in the water — as a big musky grabbed my lure the very moment it touched the surface of the water! And at the same time, I noticed another boil, about 10 feet away, made by a different musky as it shot away. I set hard, pulling back as far as I could over my head before I could feel the weight of the fish. Just the slight amount of bow that was present in my line at the moment the lure hit the water was enough to potentially negate my hookset. Fortunately, I was able to hook the fish solidly and ended up catching and releasing it. It was 44 1/2 inches long and in the 25-pound class.

The catching of this nice musky also brings to mind another fine point: Don't be afraid to fish ultra-shallow at times, especially in the darker water lakes. This 44 1/2-inch musky hit my Topper very tight to shore — in less than two feet of water! During low light conditions in the summer, or when you have exceptionally warm temperatures heating up the shallows during the spring or fall (when the water is cooler), it's common to find big muskies in extremely shallow water. But there will often be access to deeper water close by.

Two early September instances come to mind. I once was fishing a small island bar and threw my black Tally Wacker so tight to the island that I didn't expect anything to hit the lure right away. The water was less than a foot deep there! But just after my lure hit the water, WHAMMO! — I caught a near 20-pound musky. But, there did happen to be a 20-foot hole only a stone's throw away!

Another time, I got up at daybreak to fish during the early morning full moon. It was clear, calm, and very cool. The early morning fog was still hanging over the water. Walleyes were breaking the surface as I worked around the entire perimeter of a point bar, casting my black Creeper onto the bar. Beginning to reach the shallowest part of the bar, I threw my Creeper into less than two feet of water when I noticed my lure quietly sink — as if a weed had pulled it under. Naturally, I set the hook ... just in case.

It did turn out to be a fish but didn't seem very impressive at first. There wasn't even the slightest splash or boil. I thought it might be a walleye, but quickly changed my mind when I felt some slow head shaking and then the power of the fish as it swam by the boat and just kept on going. It was a musky!

It was a powerful swimmer, fighting deep the whole time and never once coming up to the surface. I realized this fish was well over 20 pounds and even had a few wild thoughts about how big this fish could be! I never saw the musky until I got it into the net; the water had a heavy

John Dettloff releases a 29-pound musky that hit a Creeper at dawn in September. Dettloff tagged this fish and five years later it was caught again — this time weighing 34 pounds.

Putting These Tips Into Practice

green algae bloom and I couldn't see anything below the surface. The fish was a solid 46 1/2-inch musky and I weighed it on my boat scale — while it was still in the net. After subtracting the weight of the net, I knew it wouldn't quite make the 30-pound mark so I tagged and released it. This 29-pound fish was my biggest musky catch at that time, September 9, 1987, and it was very cooperative, making for a successful release.

That fish evaded capture for nearly five years until one of the guests at our resort, Mike Drover, caught it within only a half mile of where I caught it. It grew to be 49 1/2 inches and weighed just over 34 pounds, a fish to be proud of and one I don't begrudge him for keeping. I released that fish for the very reason that it could grow to be a little bigger and someone else could catch it when it was of "keeping size." Many, but not all, 30-pound class muskies can survive being released and the relatively slow growth exhibited by this particular musky — only three inches and five pounds in five years — indicated that this fish probably never would have grown to be much over 40 pounds.

Just as big fish can be found in ultra-shallow water at times, as mentioned earlier, they can also be found deeper on occasion, relating closer to the edge of a shallow bar. The story of how Frenchy LaMay caught his 41-pound musky, back on July 5, 1957, not only illustrates this point, but also how crucial having just the right timing is:

It was Frenchy's first day off from guiding his friend Walter J. Roman in three weeks. After throwing a couple of sandwiches into his red plywood Chippewa boat and starting up his 7 1/2-horsepower Evinrude, Frenchy scooted away for a full day of fishing and relaxation. While casting a Super Duper in Two Boys, one of the most remote parts of the Chippewa Flowage, he caught a couple of crappies and lost a walleye. Frenchy was just diddling around, having a good, quiet time.

By late in the afternoon, the sky began to darken and he figured he'd better get out of there and head back. But the storm came too fast. While making his way out of the narrow channel that led into Two Boys, Frenchy broke a shear pin on his motor and had to sit out the rest of the storm on a stump until he could fix his motor.

Frenchy didn't know it but fate was intervening, setting in motion a chain of events or circumstances that would ultimately put him and a 40-pound-plus musky crossing paths a little later. The timing was crucial; it always is. After changing his shear pin and getting underway, Frenchy passed by Herman's Landing and made the bend heading back to Indian Trail Resort. Worried about the storm, he kept looking up at the sky. It was purple and swirling around up there! Fearing the storm would hit again and that he'd get stuck crossing the big water in his little red plywood boat, he considered turning back and waiting out the storm at Herman's. And just as he was about to turn around, he spotted four boats on Pete's Bar — all clustered together on the shallow hump. Frenchy figured, since they were out there, he might as well make a few casts, too.

Not wanting to horn in on their fishing, Frenchy stopped out deeper than usual near an old deadhead that was hung up off the edge of the bar. There was just a ripple and the water, like the sky, was purple — the weather was real "skootchie." It was about 7 or 8 p.m. His yellow Pflueger Globe made a white splash as it hit the water. Every so often he would pop the Globe slightly, giving it a little squirt. He made no more than six casts, maybe just reaching the edge of the bar, when on his second twitch a huge musky just annihilated his lure. He never had a fish hit any harder. Mud was boiling up to the surface as the musky churned the water, trying to throw the Globe.

Needless to say, Frenchy had caught the attention of the other fishermen on the bar. Upon getting the fish near the boat and into shooting range, he grabbed his pistol and shot the fish. Frenchy was nervous and shaking so much that the bullet missed its target, the musky's back, and only

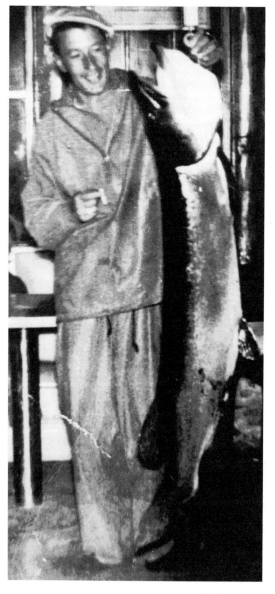

This monster was caught just after a major July storm on a Pflueger Globe by Frenchy LaMay. The musky measured 54 1/2 inches and weighed 41 pounds. The Globe has proven itself many times over as a big fish bait!

caught about two inches of the musky's belly. You want to
see a musky shoot across a bar! And with his rod held
straight up, he could feel his line billow out with his
thumb and settle back down — almost backlashing — as
the stunned musky stripped half a spool of line off his
Pflueger Supreme reel. Frenchy did manage to turn the
musky and work him back to the boat. And aiming a little
better the second time, he shot again, hitting the mark.
The musky made a furious last lunge toward the motor
and Frenchy recalled, "If he misses it, he's mine!" He did
and Frenchy brought him boatside to gaff his fine catch.
Not wanting the musky's tail to touch the boat for fear that
it might get the leverage to jump off the gaff hook,
Frenchy had to stand up high on his boat seat as he lifted
his musky in. His friend, Charlie Wolfe, called out from
one of the other boats, "How big is he Frenchy?" After
flopping the musky down and seeing that it spanned the
full width of his boat, Frenchy said, "I think it's over 30
pounds, maybe 35 pounds!"

The musky weighed in at 41 pounds and was
54 1/2 inches long, the largest recorded musky catch out
of the flowage for 1957. (A 30-pounder, with 11 pounds
to spare!) All of the fishermen of Indian Trail were in the
bar, taking shelter from the storm, when Frenchy brought
in his catch. No one was out in that storm — no one

except for Frenchy LaMay. Just think, if that storm wouldn't have been quite as threatening or if no one else would have been fishing Pete's Bar, Frenchy probably would have continued right on by without stopping to fish. Or if he hadn't sheared a pin in Two Boys' channel, the timing would have been all wrong. As Frenchy has said many times before, "Musky fishing is a game of inches."

Don't ever neglect doing an angle change with your lure once it gets near the boat. This fine point is a very important surface bait subtlety that deserves to be reiterated. This simple and key maneuver, which triggers those last minute strikes, has put many "bonus muskies" into my boat over the years.

The very first person I ever heard talk about this tactic was Frenchy LaMay, referring to an exciting experience he had almost 40 years ago with his first big musky catch.

It was on June 27, 1955, on the west end of Cranberry Bar, on the Chippewa Flowage, when Frenchy noticed a large wake trailing his orange Surf-Oreno. He twitched, popped, and sped up his lure, doing everything he could to entice a strike — but the musky wouldn't hit. The wake just kept on coming and Frenchy was soon going to run out of room. So once his lure got near the boat, Frenchy jerked his rod off to the side — doing a 90-degree angle change with his lure, alongside his boat. The musky reacted by violently slashing at the Surf-Oreno with such furor that its tail slapped into the side of Frenchy's little red plywood boat so hard that it cracked the side of his boat! After playing the fish and subduing it with one shot, Frenchy had himself (at that time) his biggest musky — a nice 26-pound fish.

That lesson has stuck in my head ever since I first heard that story almost 20 years ago. And just two years ago, in July, that angle change maneuver literally had the muskies jumping into the boat for me! I was fishing alone, on one of my nights off from guiding, casting one of my homemade Water Thumpers (a Tally Wacker-type lure) near Sand Island on the west side of the Chippewa Flowage. The

Frenchy LaMay's 90-degree boatside angle change was too much for this 26-pound musky. He caught the fish June 27, 1955.

water was calm and it was almost dusk — aha, the "bewitching hour" again! A fellow guide, Ron Bergman, and his son pulled up next to me to chit-chat. Naturally, I kept casting while we talked and, upon briefly glancing back at my lure, I noticed a nice little wake behind it. Shouting to Bergman that I had one coming, I braced myself as I prepared to do my angle change next to the boat. And when I did, the maneuver triggered an immediate strike!

A short, hard hookset drove the hooks home and the musky reacted by catapulting itself five feet up into air — almost hitting me — and coming down right into my boat! The fish amazingly landed dead center into my net, which was facing upward with the bag open, never touching the rim of the net going in! We all were laughing with amazement as I quickly measured and released it — a little jumbled up — but unharmed. It was about a 10-pounder.

Don't Be Afraid To Experiment

Between scrounging for the old classic surface baits at flea markets and visiting your favorite sport shop for their latest in topwater lures, an angler will have no problem building up a collection of topwater treasures. But, just as a premier trout fisherman finds satisfaction in tying his own flies, a very rewarding part of the sport of musky fishing is making your own lures and trying to catch muskies on them. What a great feeling it is to catch a nice-sized musky on what may be a crude looking concoction, but in reality is a "killer" lure with a sound that the muskies just can't resist.

Frenchy LaMay, well known for his "homemade" surface baits, has elevated the making of homemade lures to almost an art form. His "LeLures" — as he calls them

116

— are jewels that have set the standard in lure making. But to me, there is one surface bait that — above all others — best embodies the whole mystique of the making and using of homemade lures for musky fishing. This quintessential lure is know as "Sneaky Joe." Crude but effective, this lure is the personification of its inventor, Walter J. Roman.

Of the hundreds of thousands of fishermen who have fished the famed Chippewa Flowage since it was first created, Roman is one who is not easily forgotten. When Walt tied into a musky — any musky — there was often turmoil and Walt's voice could be heard echoing all over the flowage. If you were fishing within even a mile of him, you knew it.

Walt was a janitor for several Chicago apartment buildings and, over 30 years ago, while fixing a woman's faucet, he spied an old wooden chair in her storeroom. Being a musky fisherman, he thought that he could make several good lures out of the legs of that chair — so he cut two of them off. Bewildered, the woman later told Walt that someone had cut the legs off her chair. "What would anyone do that for?" Walt innocently asked.

Walt made a surface bait body out of a section of one of the chair legs — he put a heavy, globe-type spinner on it (slightly off-center), covered the lure with dull black

*Lure-making master Frenchy LaMay creating a new
killer surface lure.*

paint, and put two spreaders (or "set-ups," as he called
them) on the lure — each extending two treble hooks out
to the sides. The heavy, hardwood body and oversized
spinner allowed the lure to run low but still stay on the surface, making a deep-pitched, "churgling" sound. The lure
would actually sink after it soaked up a little water but, as
long as the lure was being retrieved, it would stay just on
the surface. This lure was simply known as the Chairleg,

the forerunner of the Sneaky Joe.

When Walt first brought his new creation to try on the Chippewa Flowage, during his 1965 summer vacation at Indian Trail Resort, his friend Frenchy didn't think the lure would work very well because its hooks were too conspicuous. But he became a believer when Walt caught a musky on it in one of the first spots that they fished. The musky was a wild fish, jumping several times and tangling the line around both the lure and the musky's gills during the fight. The line parted just after the fish was boated. Luckily, this new secret lure wasn't lost on its test run!

For the next four years, Walt cleaned house with his Chairleg — catching lots of fish with it and even tangling with some real brutes. Sometimes it seemed as if Walter could do no wrong with that lure. During one weekend fishing trip in August of 1966, Walt caught four muskies on his Chairleg during only 16 hours of fishing! On the first day, Walt got a 20-pounder off West Cranberry Bar with it. Later on he went back out, this time to East Cranberry Bar, and had a musky around 12 pounds jump right into his boat — chasing after the Chairleg as he was pulling it out of the water.

The next day, in his first spot, Walt caught another legal-sized musky with that same lure. And after running into his friend, Leo Petrouske, Leo told Walt that he didn't think it would be a good day because there was an east wind. (You've heard of the old saying, "When the wind blows from the east, the fish bite the least." Well, don't believe it!) Walt proved Leo wrong by going back out and nailing a 30-pounder on his Chairleg on West Cranberry!

It was the best fight that Walt ever had with a musky. When the fish hit, Walt set the hooks so hard that he lost his footing and fell over in the boat, hooking his foot onto another lure that was rigged up on one of his other rods. The fish was going crazy and Walt was cussing because he couldn't stand back up in his boat. He had to play the fish from the bottom of the boat, keeping his rod

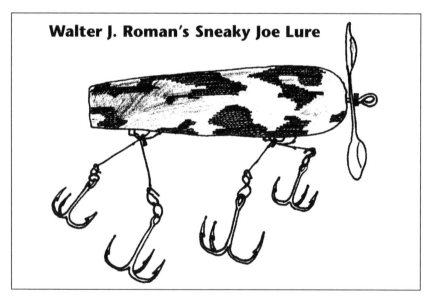

Walter J. Roman's Sneaky Joe Lure

held as high as possible. Walt finally managed to rip the hooks out of his tennis shoe with a pliers, scrambling to his feet to finish fighting the fish.

This Chairleg lure hardly ever left the end of Walt's pole after that. One day, after forgetting to retie his knot as he usually did, Walt's worn line parted on a long cast and his favorite lure sailed into the darkness and slowly sank to the bottom. So back to his original chair legs Walt went and, during the next winter, concocted a new and even better lure for the following season — Sneaky Joe!

Sneaky Joe was similar to its predecessor, but just a bit shorter and splotched with black and gold paint. This low riding lure pushed a nice big wake and made even a better sound than the Chairleg. At a slow retrieve, Sneaky Joe would make a quiet — but very deep pitched — ticking sound that penetrated deep into the water. Walt ended up dealing with more trophy muskies on this lure than most men see in a lifetime! During a 10-day streak in 1971 Walt caught seven muskies — all on his Sneaky Joe! And two of those fish were over 25 pounds. This is just when I started to develop an interest in musky fishing and I can remember how both "Walter J." and his homemade Sneaky Joe were regarded with such reverence.

The Sneaky Joe had an uncanny ability to attract big muskies. The key was that it satisfied the main charac-

Walter J. Roman with a nice 25 1/2-pound musky — one of many big Chippewa Flowage muskies that fell victim to his "Sneaky Joe" surface bait in 1971.

teristics that are important in a big fish bait: the lure rode low in the water, pushed a good wake, and made a very deep pitched sound at a slow retrieve.

Walt lost a real monster on his Sneaky Joe in August of 1972. It was drizzly, cold, and rough on the big water, so Walt tried Little Pete's Bar where it happened to be a bit more protected. A friend, Fred Hirsch, was in another boat working the same area when Walt had a tremendous "suck job" on his Sneaky Joe. The hit was so hard and loud that even Hirsch set, as a reflex. His Globe shot out of the water like it fired from a cannon, almost hitting him. For a split second Fred was baffled, until he

Don't Be Afraid To Experiment

saw Walt battling a sow! Walt had his hands full as the huge musky, well over 40 pounds, had the water foaming! But because he put too much pressure on the fish, the split rings shattered and the hooks tore right off the lure! I think I learned a few new cuss words that night — being only 10 years old at the time — after Walt had returned, beaten once again by another big 'lunge.

Before Walt passed away, he gave me his prized lure which I still use today. It's probably the ugliest lure in my tackle box, but the muskies don't seem to mind. It may not have a shiny finish, fancy airbrushed paint job, or glitzy appearance like the store bought surface baits do; but, this simple lure, made from the leg of a chair, catches fish. I wouldn't trade it for any other lure.

Oh, No! I Can't Lose That Lure!

How many musky hunters do you know who, upon getting a near 50-inch musky hooked and up to the boat, have worried more about losing their lure — than the fish itself? Who in their right mind would entertain such a notion? Well, I must admit ... I did last Labor Day. Obviously, an explanation is warranted, but not before I give you a little background on this most irresistible musky lure — my "September Globe."

But before I elaborate, one should realize that top-water musky men are indeed a different breed. For one thing, patience — something inherent in all musky hunters — is a virtue that surface bait fishermen must have a double dose of. I know many a bucktail man who has a hard time "slowing down" their presentation when using the slower retrieval surface lures. The extra time it takes to work an area with a surface lure may make some musky anglers a little restless, but the extra effort applied can often pay off in big dividends.

Also, because both lure buoyancy and sound are critical elements of a surface bait, it only stands to reason that one is likely to get more attached to these types of lures. For if you lose a favorite surface bait, you can be losing much more than just a high confidence lure. You actually can be losing an irreplaceable fish getting attractor. A properly working surface lure is like a finely tuned musical instrument — just the right sound is essential.

I acquired one such lure (one of Frenchy LaMay's custom made "magnum" black Globes) about 10 years ago. At first glance I thought this lure — being almost eight inches long, 1 1/3 inches thick, and weighing 3 ounces — might have been a bit too large. And the nearly 3 1/2-inch long, 16 gauge, stainless steel propeller that it sported looked more like it would make a good replacement prop for my trolling motor! Nevertheless, I decided to give it a try — as soon as I could find a "pool cue" to cast it with!

Several nice musky catches on this lure in September of 1985 told me that I had my hands on a good fish getter. The unique, deep-pitched, slow, chirping sound made by this lure seemed to attract a higher than usual number of big muskies and, to date, has been responsible for producing 20 legal musky catches (fish over 32 inches) averaging 18 pounds. With 15 of those catches occurring in September, I was quick to dub this pet lure my "September Globe." But — to be honest — I must confess to using it earlier in the season at times.

One such day, August 26, 1987, I shall never forget. On this day, I dealt with what could have been three different 30-pounders ... two of which were on my "September Globe"! It was a perfect musky day on the Chippewa Flowage — heavy clouds all day, warm, and calm in the morning with a moderate northeast chop during the evening.

That morning, I managed to sneak away from the resort for a half hour's fishing on the Church Bars — an area where my wife had a follow from a 30-pounder on an orange Crazy Crawler just the morning before. And, in the same spot with the same lure at the same time, 9 a.m., I brought up the same fish, 48 to 50 inches long — almost as if I willed that fish to be there. The musky had nipped at my lure three times and, on reflex, I set and pulled the lure away on the last little nip. That fish had me so shook up, concentrating on my morning resort chores was difficult.

But once evening came, I was back out on the water

Oh, No! I Can't Lose That Lure!

and, by 7 p.m., caught two average sized muskies on a krackle Globe. With the muskies obviously on a feed, I switched to my "September Globe" and headed for the fabled Pete's Bar — in search of something big. After spending over an hour working the bar, at around sundown, I felt a little tick as my Globe came across the chop — in about five feet of water. Upon setting the hook good and hard and not even moving the fish, my thoughts that I had a hold of a 30-pound plus musky were confirmed when I saw the fish make its spectacular tarpon-like jump. But, after using his raw power to open up my 4/0 hooks, the fish threw the lure.

By the time total darkness had set in, I found myself casting this same Globe on Fleming's Bar. The adrenaline was still flowing and I was wound as tight as a spring. Night fishing with surface baits ... it doesn't get any more thrilling! Just then, my Globe ticked a weed, so I gave it a short jerk to rip the weed free. Well, that maneuver — as it often does — ended up triggering one of the most explosive short hits I'd ever heard. Believe me ... this fish was big! I couldn't help but set the hooks on that one — only to launch my lure back toward my boat. My heart had about all it could stand that night!

On another occasion, August 24, 1990, Charlie Thompson, a frequent fishing buddy, and I connected with seven muskies by 9 a.m. — the largest of which was, of course, on my "September Globe." With the overcast skies, warm temperatures, and the southerly moderate chop, the handwriting was on the wall that the muskies would be on the move. At 8 a.m., on a small, shallow, sand point in no more than three feet of water, a heavy fish socked my Globe but I only caught a piece of him. My hookset rolled the musky over, allowing the fish to expose enough side to indicate that it was at least approaching the 30-pound mark.

But I may have underestimated that fish because, two weeks later, in the same area and at the same time of day, I clearly saw one of the biggest muskies of my life! Just as I cast out my Bobbie Bait, I heard a sudden rush of water near the boat as a huge musky rose up and motionlessly exposed the total length of its body. The fish was at least in the 40-pound class; but, I state that only because I am too conservative to admit that I honestly think it could have been much bigger! I'll never know if that was the same critter that took a poke at my "September Globe" two weeks earlier.

And two years later, one morning in mid-September, I guided a client to a 32 1/2-pounder on — you guessed it — that very same Globe. (This story is highlighted later in this book.) But even with the illustrious track record of successes that it has racked up during the past nine years, my "September Globe" ended up surpassing all expectations during September of 1994. Believe it or not, having an arsenal of almost equally lethal surface baits from which to choose, I hardly ever used this charmed Globe before Labor Day during the 1994 season. And every time I passed over it in my tackle box, I found myself acknowledging it with quiet reverence by thinking to myself, "Just wait until September!"

Sounds like a lure you would do almost anything to hang onto, doesn't it? Well, several events occurred in 1994 that played an important part in making me even more protective of my favorite lures and, ultimately, led me to sacrifice the capture of a near 50-incher for my "September Globe."

First, my friend and source of special-made lures, Frenchy LaMay, experienced some minor health problems which made any future lure making on his part uncertain. So all who possessed his "LeLures" began to covet them more closely.

And it was right on the heels of that news when two of my guide clients lost two of my better working LeLures. One client had a 25-pounder snatch an orange Creeper that I'd loaned him and the fish rolled and cut the line. Boy was I crushed to lose that lure! And to add insult to injury, the fish seemed to be taunting us by jumping wild-ly a short time later, showing us the lure ... but not giving it up.

And then, a couple of days before Labor Day, another client cast off my "back up" black Globe. It was dark and the lure was never recovered — even though I spent the next two days frantically searching the nearby shorelines for it. I hated to lose that lure because it was the

John Dettloff holds NFL Hall of Famer Larry Csonka's first-ever musky, taken while filming an episode of Suzuki's Great Outdoors.

Oh, No! I Can't Lose That Lure!

one Larry Csonka caught his first musky on while we were filming a musky show for ESPN's "Suzuki's Great Outdoors" earlier that summer.

Defiantly vowing to not lose any more of my precious LeLures, I decided to go fishing after the Labor Day sun had set. On the way down to my boat with a handful of lures, I noticed a resort guest and friend, Ron Heidenreich, relaxing on the dock. Knowing he hadn't seen much during the past two cold front days, I invited him to join me. We had no idea that we were about to embark on the beginning of the most incredible big fish spree that I've ever witnessed on the Chippewa Flowage!

It was the dark of the moon — the best time to night fish — clear, 58 degrees, and there was an easy northwest chop. Water temperatures were hovering around 65 degrees. "Now is the time to resurrect my killer Globe," I thought. So, smiling with an abundance of confidence, I told Ron, "This is my September Globe, you know!" And by 9:30 p.m., the lure had bagged a nice 25-pound class, 45 3/4-inch musky for me.

After a quick release of this fish, we were all charged up and ready to fish all night! Quickly shooting over to another nearby spot, we weren't there 10 minutes when ... WHAMMO! On the end of a long cast, a much bigger musky had attacked my "September Globe." Rearing back so hard on the hookset that I fell backward right into my seat, I scrambled back to my feet. The power that this fish exhibited was impressive. But after it made a wild jump, things began to go awry.

The fish began to make incredibly fast, bonefish-like, 20-yard runs. We could just hear the line ripping through the water! The minute the fish neared the boat, I saw the problem: the line was all wrapped around the fish and "lassoed" around its tail. Trembling with excitement, we knew the fish was over 48 inches and an easy 30 pounds plus. But, horrified at the prospect of losing my "September Globe" from the possibility of the line being seriously nicked, all I could think was, "My God! ... I can't lose that lure!"

In the heat of a moment like this you only have seconds to make decisions, so — fearing that I could lose both the fish and the lure at any moment — I barked at Ron, "Let's get him into the net on our first good chance!" After doing a series of violent thrashes next to the boat, the musky moved in close and — upon my direction — Ron got the fish two-thirds of the way into my net before it started going wild. Balancing on the rim of the net for five, gut wrenching seconds of complete turmoil, this 32- to 34-pound class musky finally dumped out and swam off — but, thank God, not with my Globe! Ron, distraught over this whole episode, couldn't believe my jubilation as I happily held up and kissed my Globe. "You can get more fish like that," I told him, "but you can't replace a lure like this!" What can I tell you — musky fishermen are crazy!

And during the next two weeks, my "September Globe" was to show me more big muskies than some people see in a lifetime. The next evening, September 6, while guiding Mike and Cathy Szczepanski, we raised four fish with the biggest one (at least 25 pounds) really exploding the water as it hit the Globe short. It made such an intimidating sound that Cathy had to think twice before casting back out there.

But it was the next day, September 7, that proved to be perhaps the most exciting evening of musky fishing in my life and, once again, my "September Globe" played a major role. Taking a busman's holiday for myself, I (along with Ron Heidenreich) hired Ray Blank, a fellow top notch musky guide, to guide us that evening. After guiding all summer long, it sure is nice to relax and let someone else work the boat and cater to you. I recommend hiring guides — no matter how accomplished one thinks he is. It's a treat to oneself and, with the right guide, always is worth it.

While Ray worked us along the edge of Sand Island's bar, I kept my eyes transfixed on my "September

Surface Bait Subtleties

Globe" as it slowly made its way through the light southeast chop. At 7:30 p.m. I noticed a slight wake — that only I could see — rise up behind the lure and disappear. A split second later it clobbered the Globe and shot its four-foot form out of the water like a missile. After circling deep around the boat, the fish came in close and Ray put her in the net bag. At 48 inches and 28 to 30 pounds, this musky (which we released) would normally be cause for celebration — but that would come later. We had more fishing to

John Dettloff and guide Ray Blank display Dettloff's 48-incher caught on the September Globe.

Oh, No! I Can't Lose That Lure!

do!

At 8:20 p.m., Ron had one charge his Creeper to the boat on Risberg's Bar. And with no shortage of places from which to choose, we then advanced to another spot. The endless variety of good spots that inundate the Chippewa Flowage all promise to be good musky haunts, as long as they offer ample weed growth or stumps on bars that top off at two to eight feet. Once total darkness had set in, Ron had a tremendous short hit on his Creeper that caused our collective blood pressures to rise considerably.

We could make out three other boats fishing nearby and, within five minutes, the quiet was again broken as one of them — manned by Charlie Thompson — battled a good 20-pounder. As he was landing that musky, I had on and lost a good fish on my "September Globe." And, just after that fish got off, the boat closest to us — occupied by the Szczepanskis — had a 44-incher violently attack a LeLure Fetch & Catch right next to their boat. Ray's comment, "Oh, I'm on pins and needles right now!" echoed our sentiments exactly as we realized that we were hitting into a school of big muskies.

After beating those waters to a froth for a good half hour more, Ray and I mutually decided to hit a nearby spot that nobody had been fishing. Thinking to myself, "Boy, now I can relax a bit," I didn't even get 10 casts out when a savage explosion of terrifying proportions took place on my lure. The musky hit with a killing vengeance, foaming the water for a full 10 seconds and almost totally destroying my September Globe. Even though it was 10:15 p.m. and pitch dark, all I could see was a violent spray of white water working its way toward the boat. This "Esox Tasmanian devil" had us all in oxygen debt!

After finally settling down, the musky still managed to dart around enough to keep me on my toes. By the time Ray bagged the fish, the excitement had me both physically and mentally spent! And even though this 25-pound class, 45-inch long musky had completely engulfed my Globe, after cutting the lure to pieces I amazingly was able to release the fish.

This favorite Globe of mine not only was badly mauled, having nearly half the paint stripped off of it and splinters of white cedar coming up — it almost was lost that night. For, during all the thrashing that took place, my line ended up getting severely frayed and almost parted.

By the next evening, September 8, I had my September Globe completely rebuilt and ended up having another big one (probably a 30-pound class fish) smash at it. My guide clients, the Rittmuellers, also had the same fish hit at their lure, caught a 36-incher, and helped me boat a nice hybrid musky that just couldn't resist my lucky Globe.

Each day continued to be action packed during the very stormy week that followed, with the black Globe seemingly keeping the muskies' interest. And when the dust had finally cleared, our little fishing camp ended up producing a record 61 legal muskies in 12 days with only two fish kept and many fish respectable in size! From September 5 to 21 alone, the Chippewa Flowage produced seven 30-pound class muskies, one 34-pound 10-ounce musky and two 37-pound class muskies!

The crowning glory of the month occurred for me on September 21, one of the final "summer period" days we were to have. It was overcast with a slight southeasterly breeze and still surprisingly warm. The fact that water temperatures had risen to nearly 70 degrees by then probably was the reason that the muskies had been on such a prolonged September feed. My wife, Paulette, wanting to get in on this musky bonanza, enlisted me to guide her to a big musky that evening. Not intending to cast myself, I planned on rowing her through the spots.

At around 7 p.m., after really working over a small sand bar, Paulette asked if we were done with the spot yet. I told her that it needed three more casts to be covered, so she told me to finish it off. And believe it or not, on my third and final cast, when my September Globe neared the boat I saw the water drop down and then rise up behind the lure — about a half a second before a horse of a fish nailed it! A short, hard hookset and quick press of my freespool had me ready for this four-foot long bundle of green lightning to wildly go thrashing away from the boat.

John Dettloff holds a 48-inch, 30-pound-plus musky before releasing it. The fish hit his September Globe on September 21, 1994.

Oh, No! I Can't Lose That Lure!

One of the most exciting and enjoyable trophy muskies that I've ever caught, this fish did just about every type of acrobatic maneuver that one could hope for. At one point I could see that it had my Globe completely engulfed, but after the fish threw a pailful of water on Paulette with its tail as it took off, I noticed that the lure had changed its position when I finally worked the fish back to the boat for Paulette to net.

Now only lightly hooked in the jaw, the lure was easily shaken free once Paulette got the fish into the net. Measuring 48 inches in length, this well built 31- to 32-pound musky made a great release. My September Globe no worse for the wear, produced a 39-inch musky and brought up several other nice ones the very next day.

Now maybe you better understand why this particular musky nut has been so paranoid about losing his September Globe.

Let Fate Be
Your Guide

Some of the biggest muskies that people have caught were caught — not because the angler purposely was following a specific plan of action — but because fate smiled upon them at just the right time. There are scores of examples that illustrate this to be true in the sport of musky fishing, proving that an angler just never knows when, or how, his time will come.

Some musky anglers put so much effort into their quest for a big fish that they begin to get burned out and discouraged when they can't satisfy their goal. A person shouldn't get too hung up on having to catch that one big fish within a pre-established time frame. It can ruin one's love of the sport. If you're meant to catch a big musky, you will. Persistence will guarantee it. And it doesn't hurt to let fate guide you.

Even the best musky fishermen can't predict when

that time will come; so you must be ready at all times. No matter what the circumstances are, it is possible that the very next cast you make could get you the biggest musky of your life!

One of Wisconsin's best known and most productive musky guides, Tony Rizzo, caught the biggest musky of his life while he was sitting on shore eating lunch, taking a break from his more traditional fall methods. Rizzo knew that there was a chance he could catch a decent fish if he soaked a few suckers off shore, while breaking for lunch — but he probably never dreamed he would catch a 41-pounder doing it!

Another time, in August of 1973, Frenchy LaMay was heading over to the Chippewa Flowage's Pork Barrel Island when he noticed, along the way, that Little Pete's Bar had no boats on it. But because Little Pete's had been dead, and Pork Barrel had a known active big musky on it, Frenchy never intended to hit Little Pete's that night. But upon discovering that a couple of other boats had gotten to Pork Barrel ahead of him, Frenchy turned his boat around and decided to hit Little Pete's anyway. It was one of the few spots in that vicinity that had no boats on it.

Fate had guided Frenchy well that night, for he ended up taking a huge musky, just under 40 pounds, on an orange Topper on that very spot! Just think, if those other boats hadn't beaten Frenchy to Pork Barrel first — he never would have caught that big musky.

Kismet also lead my friend Charlie Thompson to the biggest musky catch of his lifetime. It was during early July of 1983. Charlie fished all evening with no action, finishing up on the flowage's Fleming's Bar. It was pitch dark and time to call it quits. Just another very pleasant, but fishless, evening. Well, fate was about to change that!

Upon turning the key to start his motor, Charlie was perturbed to discover that the motor wouldn't start. Click, click was all he heard. There was some sort of electrical problem. Upon glancing at his depthfinder, Charlie saw that he was still on the bar — so he decided to throw a few more casts. And after only one cast with his black Tally Wacker, — WHAMMO — he caught a 34-pound musky! In all the excitement, Charlie had forgotten about his motor trouble and amazingly, when he turned the key to start his motor so he could race home with his big fish, his motor started!

Fate has guided me so many times to muskies that, now if for any reason, circumstances force me to change my fishing game plan — I go with it and don't even try to fight it. I can remember one such case vividly:

It was on the morning of the 15th of September in 1992, when I was guiding Dennis Lempicki and his friend,

Victor. Even though the musky action had been very slow that week, I was still excited about the morning — it was warm, there was a light southeast chop on the water, and there were heavy, overcast skies. A perfect musky day! My game plan was to row my two clients along the entire south edge of an island so they could cover the scattered shallow cabbage weeds along the shore.

Casting beyond a small root off one corner of the island, the winds of des-

Charlie Thompson proved that night fishing with surface lures can be deadly for big fish. This 34-pound beauty was caught on a Tally Wacker.

tiny ended up blowing Dennis' line over the root. Being forced to row the boat up to the root so I could free his line, I now was faced with changing my original game plan. For to row back out, against the wind, and reposition my boat to where it was would take a little effort. So, on the spur of the moment, I decided to let the wind push me just a bit farther so we would be in perfect position to fish the next island over — a spot that I had no intention on fishing until later on.

The, perhaps clairvoyant, notion popped into my head that, maybe there was a reason that Dennis' snag ended up making me change my game plan. So with renewed confidence, I held the boat off the edge of a shallow sand bar that extended from the island, instructing my companions to keep casting over the shallow weeds. And as I became satisfied with the coverage of each section of the bar, I moved the boat a bit further so they could cast to a slightly different section.

I'll never forget how violent and disruptive the strike was as a big musky snatched Dennis' black Globe from the waves. The water erupted as the fish thrashed and created an impressive turbulence on the surface. The brute emerged from beneath the commotion and glided off to the right. I could see how even a good fisherman could have thought this was a 40-pound fish. It looked so impressive upon my first glimpse of it! And, down he went, head shaking and then waddling away with power.

After turning and coming back up to the surface, it showed itself even better the next time. It still looked like it could be a 35-pound-plus fish. Taking a deep breath, I told Dennis, "You've got a big fish! You've got him! Relax and don't overpressure it. If he runs, let him go but keep a tight line!" Excited and poised with the net, I got ready to take

John Dettloff's September Globe produced this 32 1/2-pounder for Dennis Lempicki (right).

advantage of my first good chance to net this beast. And on the musky's third time near the boat, I was able to get her into the net. Victor helped me haul the fish aboard and Dennis had himself a beautiful 32-pound 6-ounce musky!

Fate had guided us well, putting us on the path to catching a musky that we could have easily not even fished for that morning!

Releasing Muskies

U p until the early 1970s, release percentages consistently remained below 10 percent and the few conservation-minded souls who occasionally released a musky were often met with shades of disbelief from others. After all, a well-earned musky catch represented good eating to most anglers back then. Remember, many fishermen from that era were products of the Depression and to throw away food just somehow went against the grain. Before the release concept could come of age, the time had to be right.

But in the meantime, some organizations began to look at the big picture and realized that encouraging the release of some muskies and recommending a more conservation-minded harvest would help to sustain a quality musky fishery into the future. The Muskellunge Club of Wisconsin, founded in 1953, was one of the first organizations to introduce the release concept to the musky angling public — some 40 years ago. But it wasn't until the mid-1970s that the release concept began to be widely embraced by the public.

A rapidly growing new club at that time, Muskies, Inc., took the release concept and made it a high priority to heavily promote this practice. I can remember catching my first really big musky at about this time, when the release program was just beginning to catch on with the smaller fish. The year was 1977 and I remember it like it were yesterday when Joe Jasek guided me to a beautiful fish just shy of 25 pounds — truly a memorable experience. As Joe netted my prized fish, hauled it aboard, and subdued it with his club, he jokingly said with a wink in his eye, "Oh, I'm sorry, I forgot to ask you if you wanted to release this one." We all had a good laugh as we knew he was joking. After all, who in their right mind would throw back such a big fish?

But during the coming years, an amazing momentum was to build that would take the release concept further than perhaps anyone had ever dreamed. After seeing almost immediate improvements in their musky fisheries, anglers began to release even more and bigger fish. And by the 1990s, volunteer release percentages had approached the 90 percent mark, 20- to 30-pound class muskies were commonly being released, and even some 40-pound class fish were being thrown back — something unheard of in the 1970s.

So here we are, just a few short years away from the close of the century — and closing it on a very positive note indeed, as far as the status of most of our musky fisheries goes. Angler overharvest is no longer a serious threat to most of our waters now and, as long as we keep our lakes and rivers free from pollution, the "good old days" will continue. The release ethic that has so swept through the musky range like a prairie fire is now deeply embedded into the fabric of our sport, guaranteeing that we will be handing over to the musky anglers of the next century one of the healthiest musky fisheries ever!

People hear so much about the release program and usually have good intentions about releasing most of their muskies. Unfortunately, there still isn't enough instruction made available on how to do it properly and most efficiently. And, with all of the surface bait subtleties that are presented in this book, you may want to bone up on your release procedures — because I have a feeling you'll be catching more muskies than you'll know what to do with!

When releasing a musky — especially a big one — there are certain key factors that make for a successful release. And the bigger a musky is, the older it is, and the more care that should be administered if the fish is to survive being released. It should be noted that some big muskies just are not releaseable. But, if a systematic release game plan is adhered to, most big muskies (25 to 40 pounds or better) can be successfully released.

The following four rules should be followed by anyone intending to release a musky:

1. Don't "play out" a musky any longer than you

Well-known musky historian Larry Ramsell releases a 33- or 34-pound Georgian Bay musky to fight again. The fish was caught on a surface bait — a Hi-Fin Twin Teasertail.

Surface Bait Subtleties

need to.

If a big musky is played out too long, its chances of surviving being released can drop considerably. Huge muskies are often old and nearing the end of their life cycles. They should not be played to exhaustion. And because you can land a big musky more quickly with a net than by using any other method, the proper use of a net can maximize a big musky's survivability. Conversely, hand landing a big musky requires a maximum amount of "playing time" and can weaken the fish to a greater degree.

2.) Leave both the net and the fish in the water.

The net acts only as a "holding tank" and should never be brought into the boat with a musky in it that's going to be released. Otherwise, major entanglements and physical injury to the fish are likely to occur.

3.) If the musky is very solidly hooked and it may take a long time to remove the hooks, cut them with a bolt cutter.

This is self explanatory. Don't fool around for a long time trying to remove your hooks from a musky that you want to release. Just cut them off and save yourself a lot of time.

4.) A musky that is going to be released should only be out of the water for a minimum amount of time — only for about half a minute.

Dr. Noland Eidsmoe holds a nice 21-pounder caught by the late George Mattis, accomplished outdoor writer. Note the old Bon-net surface lure hooked to the fish. Nice muskies like this were harder to find at the time of its catch — 1958 — than now, as the catch and release ethic has greatly improved musky fisheries.

This is a critical rule of thumb to follow when releasing a big musky — a rule that many of us are guilty of breaking. When we catch a musky, we get caught up in

153

Surface Bait Subtleties

the excitement of the moment and often lose track of time. Both novice and expert anglers alike should make a conscious effort to not have a musky out of the water too long. My rule of thumb is to try not to have a musky out of the water any longer than I can hold my breath — that's less than one minute for most of us!

These are the basic rules that I try to follow when I'm releasing my muskies. It's good to rehearse a release procedure ahead of time in your mind, to be best prepared for when you have to use it. I have released hundreds of muskies using this game plan and believe me — it works.

While I strongly encourage anglers to try to release most of their muskies, I certainly don't expect them to release all of them. If a person catches a musky which is, to them, a personal trophy and one they would like to keep and mount, I don't think they should feel guilty about doing so — but should be proud of their great angling accomplishment. The occasional harvest of a musky here and there isn't going to hurt our waters, as long as it is done in a conservation-minded manner. I always say, "You don't have to release 100 percent of your muskies (over 90 percent would be nice), but make sure that 100 percent of the muskies that you do release, survive."

Epilogue

A method not for the weak of heart, surface bait fishing for muskies is both easier and less tiring for the occasional angler and highly productive on a wide variety of waters. Whether you're just beginning to take up musky fishing or are an accomplished musky hunter who, up until now, may have overlooked the effectiveness of surface lures, surface bait fishing is certainly worth trying.

While the catching of a muskellunge is considered by many to be one of the most rewarding of all freshwater angling feats, the taking of a musky with a surface lure is without a doubt the most thrilling of all the angling methods to employ. Fishing bucktails, jerkbaits, crankbaits, livebait, and trolling all are indeed exciting in their own rights, but the heart-stopping, explosive strikes and the spectacular aerial acrobatics that frequently follow, truly make topwater musky angling the ultimate thrill in musky fishing. As my musky fishing mentor, Frenchy LaMay, seasoned veteran of 49 years, once said, "I'd rather catch one big musky on a surface bait than several big ones on underwater lures! Nothing can match the thrill of seeing them come and hit your lure."

Sage Advice From A Musky Fishing Legend

"If you're casting a bait all day long and you don't get nothin', you may get kind of sour at everybody and the world and yourself. So change baits often and it will stir up the enthusiasm and will keep you from going to shore and making coffee. And if you've got the bait in the water, your percentage is better than if you're settin' over on a log someplace smokin' a cigarette.

"What makes a person a champion musky fisherman? Well, it's like Joe Louis used to say, it's mostly luck. And, of course, what makes anybody catch a lot of any kind of fish is being out there fishing. Actually, I fished more than I should have. I was a businessman and I should have been home working probably but, like any fisherman, I'd rather be out fishing.

"As far as when the best time to go fishing is, I've caught big muskies during all times of the year — so, I don't know what to say. My experience is ... that when you get the urge to go musky fishing, go out and you're liable to catch one."

— LOUIE SPRAY